Aren't You Forgetting Someone?

Essays from My Mid-Life Revenge

Kari Lizer

RUNNING PRESS

PHILADELPHIA

Running Press
Hachette Book Group
1290 Avenue of the Americas, New York, NY 10104
www.runningpress.com
@Running_Press

Printed in China

First Edition: April 2020

Published by Running Press, an imprint of Perseus Books, LLC, a subsidiary of Hachette Book Group, Inc. The Running Press name and logo is a trademark of the Hachette Book Group.

The Hachette Speakers Bureau provides a wide range of authors for speaking events. To find out more, go to www.hachettespeakersbureau.com or call (866) 376-6591.

The publisher is not responsible for websites (or their content) that are not owned by the publisher.

Print book cover and interior design by Frances J. Soo Ping Chow
Cover photos copyright © GettyImages
Author photo credit: Peter Konerko

Library of Congress Control Number: 2019953643

ISBNs: 978-0-7624-6933-8 (hardcover), 978-0-7624-6934-5 (ebook)

LSC-C

10 9 8 7 6 5 4 3 2 1

For Annabel, Elias, and Dayton—I forgive you for leaving me to go live your lives.

The Essays

Alexa, Is Everything Going to Be Okay?

At eleven years old, I got my first job at the Lazy J Ranch, where suburban teenaged girls boarded their show ponies and I shoveled horseshit. I didn't get paid, but for each four hours of mucking, I was allowed to ride Squaw, the twenty-two-year-old cancer-ridden paint mare, around the perimeter of the stables—limited only to a slow walk because of her deteriorating condition. It was a good job because it was a horrible job, motivating me to find better jobs, ride better horses, work for better people, and make real money. Since then, every phase of my life, fueled by outrage, injustice, and an inappropriate sense of humor, has been a powerful motivator to propel me to the next, better phase of my life.

My underappreciated high school theater geek self was determined to show the popular crowd how woefully they underestimated me, which sent me to Hollywood to pursue my

1

dreams of professional acting. It was the 1980s, and Hollywood was more wet T-shirt contest than meritocracy for actresses in their twenties, driving me to expand my reach into writing parts for myself. Writing parts for myself made me hungry to write parts for actors better than me and led me to full-time writing. Becoming a full-time writer educated me about how hard it was to be a woman and a comedy writer, and there I was, back to shoveling shit, but motivated to create my own opportunities. And then came motherhood. The most powerful motivator of all. I suddenly cared about owning a car that didn't die on the side of the 101 Freeway. Poverty was no longer my badge of honor, and I didn't long to reside in a house in a neighborhood that screamed, "Artists live here!" My priorities had shifted. My character had transformed.

When I became the dreaded double hyphenate in the school drop-off line at my kid's elementary school—divorced-working-mom—the Mommy Wars fueled my fire for a few good years. The stay-at-home moms criticized the working moms. The working moms sneered at the yoga-pants moms. The wet-ponytail moms whispered about the Drybar-blowout moms. The no-vaccine moms were the enemies of the Happy Meal moms. A couple of the moms felt fine about themselves, but nobody liked them. We moms should have banded together, of course, because no matter how much we did, it was a pretty thankless task.

I was so busy some of those days—between mothering, writing on other people's TV shows, then eventually running my own show, waking up at 4:00 a.m. to bake cupcakes from scratch so I didn't feel the burning shame of store-bought baked goods— that I would find myself standing up halfway through peeing, declaring to no one as I yanked up my pants, "I don't have time for this." Meanwhile, it seemed to me a dad could show up for one midday assembly and have the science wing named after him in appreciation.

I had this sense that if I didn't do everything perfectly, the bottom would drop out: jobs would be lost, kids wouldn't go to college, people would die! It was all on me. It was a feeling I recognized in other mothers—I saw it in their eyes when they forgot a permission slip or realized their kid was the only one without the regulation socks on the club soccer team. I saw them at work, pretending to have read the chain of emails that had been filling up their inbox since dawn. There was no such thing as balance. No middle. Until now. This middle age. This indefinable in-between. When I'm mostly finished caring for my children and looking down the barrel of wiping my parents' asses. It's an odd time—tender and aimless and mean . . . menopause kicking in as the kids walk out the door. To have the people you love most in the world go away when your emotions are as unpredictable as a Hollywood career for a woman in her fifties. Finding my voice, which can only come with age and perspective, just when I have no one left to talk to.

And then the world decided to go crazy with me. Adding mind-blowing insult to soul-crushing injury, the fall I dropped my third and final child at college was also the fall that Donald Trump was elected to the White House. That fall, as I drove down Interstate 93 in New Hampshire, just before the election, when the outcome was still inconceivable, I had a bumper sticker on the back of my car with a picture of Donald Trump that read, "Does this ass make my car look fat?" because I thought it was funny. Heading south through the White Mountains on the mostly empty highway, I was suddenly cut off by a jacked-up pickup driven by a forty-ish white man. As he ran me out of my lane, he screamed out his open window, "I hope you die, cunt!" Shaken, I pulled off to the side of the road. That would be the first time of many to come that I felt something had been unearthed: some deep misogyny I had missed or forgotten about or ignored until it poked up its ugly head at Hillary. Later, as the #MeToo movement kicked into gear, I found myself spending a lot of time on the side of the road, wondering whether we were going backward or forward or just blowing up. And now I'm in a bad fucking mood.

I'm doing what I can emotionally, nutritionally, technologically, and medically to intervene—I'm rubbing the estrogen/progesterone/testosterone creams into my inner thigh as rigorously as I can, cancer be damned, but there aren't enough hormones on earth to offset the outrage and disappointment I feel in the country, the genders, the world, because I'm just so fucking disappointed in everyone as, I guess, you know . . . a mother. I can't even eat my feelings anymore since one deeply unkind thirty-year-old nutritionist-slash-lifestyle-coach got me off bread by shaming me for what she described as my "wheat belly."

So I'm left sitting on my couch in my pussy hat, starving to death, screaming at the TV, cheering on the Justice Department and the judicial committees and Nancy Pelosi, waiting for life to be fair.

I find myself relying more and more on my Alexa, perched on the kitchen counter: "Alexa, what's the temperature? Alexa, is Mary Tyler Moore still alive? Alexa, is everything going to be okay?"

And Alexa answers, "The current temperature is seventy-three degrees. Mary Tyler Moore died January 25, 2017. I wouldn't count on it."

A friend suggested I get out of the house. Get around people. The isolation, she said, was making me weird. She said it was no good to sit home and stew. So I went to a friend's game night, where we were supposed to bring a potluck dish for running charades. I brought a vegetarian stew. While we waited for the fun to begin, there was a thoughtful conversation among

5

thoughtful liberals about how one deals with the problem of sexual harassers, perverts, and predatory power mongers without sweeping up some good guys in the process. I blurted out, "Who gives a shit? Where were the good guys when Harvey was opening his robe to ingénues in hotel rooms? When Les Moonves had a woman on the payroll for blowjobs on demand while he was fucking with my life's work? I'll tell you where they were—keeping their mouths shut, kissing their asses, hitching their wagons to those assholes' stars. Personally, I'm in favor of a good old-fashioned prairie castration."

My charades team fell silent, so I went on to explain (as if their silence was because they had questions regarding the technicalities of the prairie instead of my unfortunate rage burst). "See, when they don't have surgical instruments on the range to geld the rams, they take a thick rubber band, wrap it around the base of the scrotum, and leave it there. It cuts off the circulation. It's incredibly painful for the first few days as the balls swell up to the size of grapefruits then eventually turn black, until they finally fall off altogether. I'd like to watch Harvey's balls drop to the floor."

"You've thought about this," one man who didn't know me, and didn't want to, finally said as he protectively crossed his legs.

"Yeah. I have," I told him, unblinking, without the hint of a smile.

"But you're kidding, right?"

"Sure," I said, "I'm kidding."

"Oh. Okay. I heard you were funny."

Then we started the game. Where it didn't get better.

I got *Les Misérables* for my charades clue, and I just stood there, motionless, while my team yelled at me, "What does it rhyme with?"

Nothing I could think of.

"Act it out!"

I couldn't.

"How many syllables?"

I couldn't even count. Finally, after what seemed like a very long time, we heard a cheer from the other room as the opposing team won the round. My team didn't tell me it was okay, good try.

I believe I've become unsuitable for mixed company.

I didn't stay for another round, and all the way home, my party shame grew.

I don't hate men! I know too many spectacular ones—including the two I birthed myself. As I walked into my empty house, I wondered what would become of me. I might live another forty years. Why did I quit smoking?

I can't escape the continuous MSNBC news feed that does nothing to reassure me about the fact that cheaters are prospering all over the place and nice girls are finishing last. I'm getting into one-sided arguments in my bathroom mirror with Betsy DeVos and Woody Allen. Is this really the next, better phase? I have too much fight and no designated enemy. Or is everybody my enemy?

I laid down on the couch and called out, "Alexa, how many syllables in *Les Misérables*?" While she was thinking, I heard a text come in. It was from the dark-haired woman on my charades team. The one who was sitting at the end of the couch. She was about my age, and I think she was a fashion photographer or a lesbian or a chef. I had thought she was trying to kill me with her eyes. She was one of those charade savants who guessed *The Iliad* when the only clue given so far was "a book." She wore clothes that looked like they came from Japan and had a haircut that did what she wanted it to. Her text said, "Hey. Sorry you left. It helps to know other people are going crazy too. We're in this together. Try to breathe."

I sat for a moment, so strangely and instantly comforted by the solidarity of a woman I didn't know. Breathe, she said. I'm going to try that. I called out to the empty room, "Alexa, how do I breathe?"

Cry It Out

In the summer of 1995, a few things happened: my twins, Annabel and Elias, were born; O. J. Simpson was on trial; and many new parents and their pediatricians were clinging breathlessly to Dr. Richard Ferber's book *How to Solve Your Child's Sleep Problems*. Dr. Ferber's method of getting your child to fall asleep on its own became known as *Ferberizing*. Most of the new mothers I knew at the time were desperately on the lookout for someone who knew more than we did about raising children, which was everyone. We were inexperienced, insecure, and easily shamed by experts. La Leche League, the advocacy group for breastfeeding, told us if we couldn't nurse our newborns, we failed; the yogi on La Brea told us if we used an epidural during birth, we failed; and Dr. Ferber told us if we didn't get those babies to develop healthy sleep associations, not only had we failed, but our children would fail for the rest of their lives! Millions of sleep-deprived parents all over the world, desperate for answers to their sleepless nights and zombie days, bought Dr. Ferber's book and gave his method a try. Most people I knew, including myself, didn't actually read the whole thing—we couldn't keep our eyes open long enough—but we got the gist: in order to sleep train your child, you must give them healthy bedtime rituals and arm them with the ability to self-soothe. The habit of continually running to your baby's side the minute you heard even the smallest squeak, scooping them up, sticking them on the boob or bottle, rocking them in the chair, driving them around in the car, or placing their infant seat on the vibrating dryer until finally surrendering and taking them into your bed where you would let them sleep attached to your breast like they were sleeping in a vat of chocolate so you could finally close your eyes was no damn good.

You were setting your child up for a lifetime of quick fixes and dependency on external salves to their internal stresses. The Ferber method promised to be quick and easy: establishing a bedtime routine, then letting your child fuss without running to soothe him or her for a predetermined and ever-increasing length of time until that baby learned to settle on his or her own and fall back to sleep without you. Dr. Ferber scoffed at the idea that this was a "cry it out" method, as some people accused. The time you left your baby to cry was a mere three minutes at the outset—hardly torture—then increasing to five, ten, maybe fifteen minutes at the longest. But within a week, he assured, you would have a baby who could get herself back to sleep without your harmful interventions, a self-soother who would take this important skill from the crib and into the world and the time when you wouldn't be there to solve her every problem for her. You would not be setting your child up with a crippling dependency on you or anything that promised instant relief the minute she felt a twinge of discomfort (read: heroin).

In the first few months of my twins' lives, I had probably already ruined them. It was the beginning of the twenty-four-hour news cycle, and I was obsessed with the O. J. trial. Every picture of my newborn babies also has Marcia Clarke or Johnny Cochran lurking in the background on the television set. The nursery, which my husband, Jack, and I had painted a sunny yellow with a "cow jumping over the moon" wallpaper border, was furnished with two matching cribs with custom linens and visually stimulating, brain-expanding black-and-white mobiles that stood untouched where they'd been assembled the month before the twins' arrival.

Annabel and Elias had spent every night in bed with me, mostly because breastfeeding twins is simply a matter of survival. There is no time for luxuries like feeding schedules or parenting strategies, and as far as Dr. Ferber's warning that my children could suffer separation anxiety later in life, that meant nothing to me. I was pretty sure there would be no "later in life" because these babies were going to kill me. The thought of sending these ravenous creatures off to college seemed so far away he might as well have talked to me about the time when I would want to have sex again. It was like science fiction. There was no place for modesty or even dignity in those early days. The minute I snapped up my size 38 triple H nursing bra from one feeding, the other baby would be ready to go, so pretty soon I stopped bothering. I didn't even wear a shirt.

Jack's relatives, who had always had the annoying habit of just barging into our house unannounced, learned quickly to knock or risk seeing things that couldn't be unseen—like me resting cool cabbage leaves on my bosoms to draw out the heat and pressure of the overwhelming milk supply while sitting on a hemorrhoid donut, shoveling food into my mouth because I had never been so hungry in my life and it felt as if those creatures were sucking out my marrow. I eventually discovered the only way I could eat in peace was in my car. The drive-through meal became my savior, the twins buckled into their car seats while I feasted on twenty-four-hundred-calorie double cheeseburgers in the parking lot. In-N-Out Burger even offered a very civilized lap placemat. This was our existence for four blurry, beautiful months. My babies and I stared into each other's eyes, ate on demand, slept when we could, showered very little, and cocooned ourselves inside the very small world of getting to know you.

But at four months, reality crashed in because I had to go back to work. Since I worked on a television writing staff that consisted of all men, only one of them married, I knew I had to get my shit together. Seeing me in my current condition could emotionally scar the sweet young guys I worked with. No reason for them to know the cruel details of the early days of parenthood until they had to. As it was, the mechanical sounds and dairy farm whooshing coming from my office at lunchtime from the breast pump were probably going to alter their enjoyment of their catered Universal commissary lunch. And the bottles of breast milk in the communal fridge marked "Kari's boob juice" was undoubtedly enough education. I'm not saying it wasn't good for them, but I didn't need to overdo it. I also had to give the showrunners confidence that I was up to the task of returning to my job, especially since I had departed for maternity leave in a bit of haste. I'd finished only twenty-three pages of my thirty-two-page script that was due. I had a cast on my arm from tripping on the stairs on the way into work one day, breaking my wrist when I reached out to stop from falling on my enormous, baby-filled middle. It was almost a hundred degrees in the San Fernando Valley every day, I was nearing two hundred pounds, and there was a rash where my thighs rubbed together that could only be alleviated with a grease-like lubricant meant for old people with diabetic feet. I finally waddled into my bosses' office, threw the twenty-three pages on their desk, and said, "I'm sorry. This is all I got. I have to go home and have some babies."

So now, coming back, I needed to work twice as hard, be twice as good as my nonlactating brethren. I couldn't burst into tears during table reads. I had to woman up. What that meant was these twins were going to have to let me sleep more than fifteen minutes at a stretch all night long. So I agreed to try to Ferberize them.

I told Jack I didn't think I could do it; I couldn't put them in their cribs and listen to them cry without going to them. He agreed this was on him. "The first time is only three minutes," he reminded me. "That's nothing." He promised we would just go for a three-hour night and work our way up to a full night's sleep.

We brought them into their room and laid them down in their cribs, and holding back tears, I told Annabel and Elias I loved them as if I were saying goodbye for the last time. And then I walked away. I went into the bedroom and listened on the baby monitor. I heard Jack say, "Good night, guys. You're going to be okay. We're right here. You're not alone," as the book instructed.

I thought to myself, *They don't speak English. You could be saying, "Mom and I are going on a Caribbean cruise. Try not to mess up the house while we're gone. We never loved you."*

Then I heard his footsteps as he walked away. Then I heard him close the door. At first, there was stunned silence. I burst into tears thinking about their confused little faces. I missed them. Then Elias started to wail. I jumped up from the bed, but Jack was in the doorway. He held up the timer in his hand. Then Annabel joined in the wailing, summoning me. Milk began pouring from my breasts in sympathy. I held a pillow to my chest. Jack suggested maybe I should go where I couldn't hear them. I said no. I needed to hear them. I needed to suffer. Now they were hysterical. I writhed on the bed in actual physical pain; it was unbearable. Finally, after what seemed like five hours, the timer went off. "Hurry!" I said. And Jack ran to them.

I clutched the baby monitor. I heard Jack go into their room. Their crying didn't pause. He didn't pick them up—that was the rule. He just yelled over their screams, "You're okay. It's bedtime. You're not alone!" It seemed to me their wailing got louder when they realized that was all they were going to get.

There was a short hiccup pause in their hysterics when he patted their backs as recommended, and then, once again, I heard their bedroom door close. The twins went apeshit with outrage. I could tell Elias was doing that kind of crying where his entire face turned purple and his limbs were shaking. Finally, after another minute of this torture, I had a thought: *Fuck. This.* I jumped up from the bed and ran down the hallway. Jack intercepted me and tried to stop me, saying, "It's only five minutes this time." I would have killed him if I had to. Like, I would have stuck my thumbs into the soft part of his throat and squeezed the life out of him. I think he sensed this and let me pass.

Every maternal cell in my body rejected the premise that for four months you teach those baby brains, "When you call me, I'll be there"—growing those synapses in a way that lets them trust that for the rest of their lives, there is someone who thinks about them, worries about them, lets them know, "I've got you." Then, at four months, when it can't even be explained to them, I'm suddenly supposed to change the rules and say, "You're on your own, kid." *Sure,* I thought. *If I keep this up, no doubt they will stop crying eventually.* I'm sure Dr. Ferber was right about that, but when they did, I was also certain, as the mother of these two, they would stop because they would have given up. I could break them like people break horses of their willfulness and need—but that night I declared, "I don't care if they're sleeping in our bed until they're twenty-five years old; I'm not doing this. Dr. Ferber can suck my dick."

Dr. Ferber, I know you're a Harvard-educated shrink and I have a high school education and was fired from McDonald's for fainting at the french fryer. But you didn't spend two years trying to conceive them, drinking dried bugs and mud from the Chinese acupuncturist, and turning sex into homework. You're not the one with scabs on your nipples and scars on your once-flat stomach.

And for the first time in my life, I was not going to defer to a white man with a superior education. For the first time in my life, I was going to trust my own instincts.

Motherhood was about to make me fearless instead of insecure. It was about to change me as a person. It was my job to protect them, and if Dr. Richard Ferber had been standing in that hallway, I would have happily killed him too. Not everyone needs to become a parent to grow up. But I did. The fierceness that being a mother brought out in me was new. I sold myself out on a regular basis before that, but those six-pound evil geniuses gave me something to fight for.

They never learned to sleep in their own beds, and when my next baby, Dayton, came along two and a half years later, the sleeping routine became a nightlong dance: lying down with Annabel and Elias on a bed in one room until they slept; then moving into my bed with Dayton until Annabel or Elias woke up, realized I was missing, and called out for me; trudging down the hallway to lie back down until they slept again—until Dayton realized I ditched him; then scurrying back to bed with Dayton until Annabel or Elias realized I had abandoned them. All night. Every night. Until it was time to go to work in the morning. And it meant I couldn't go out of town, but there was nowhere I wanted to go. Going to work and leaving them with nannies during the week was brutal, so nighttime belonged to them. Period. It was how I overcorrected for long hours in the writer's room when I couldn't get home for dinner. I was well aware that my working mother's guilt was driving my parenting choices. And I was okay with that. I believe in a guilty conscience. I think guilt makes people behave better.

I saw a lot of parents who could have stood to have a slightly more active conscience where their kids were concerned. Not that I judge.

I was warned that my behavior would bite me in the ass when it came time to send them to pursue their independence. I was told they would cling to me like ring-tailed lemurs when I tried to drop them off at preschool or if at some point I ever developed an interest in leaving my house without them. But they didn't have separation issues.

In fact, the little fuckers walked away that first day of preschool as if I were their taxi driver. They unlatched their fingers from mine, waved goodbye, and skipped off into the sunset. "Okay!" I yelled after them. "Have fun at school! Don't worry; Mommy will be right here when you're done. I'm right here. You're not alone!" I reassured no one because they had disappeared onto the climbing structure without looking back.

I looked at the kids on the bench outside the Red Room at the Country School, their heads buried into their parents' necks, nails digging into their arms. One mom told me she had to sit on that bench outside the classroom for three weeks. Another had to stay so long she finally just took a job at the school. I would have given anything for one of those needy kids. But mine never struggled with summer camps or school trips. I was never the parent called to pick my weeping child up from sleepovers in the middle of the night like Dr. Ferber promised. I knew one lucky parent with a kid so paralyzed with social anxiety he couldn't attend any of the elementary science camp sleepovers unless she was a chaperone.

It used to drive me crazy when people said, "You know the days are long, but the years are short." But now here I am with two babies legal to drink and one legal to draft—who I still wouldn't let cry in five-minute increments.

They don't sleep in my bed anymore. And they won't let me sleep in theirs. My marriage didn't last—shut up—it wasn't all my fault. And the kids aren't around very much these days—no goddamn separation issues there. When I said to them, "It's weird, this middle-age thing," they comforted me by saying, "You're not middle aged. It's pretty unlikely you're going to live to a hundred and ten."

Sometimes I miss them, and sometimes I don't. Those first nights alone, when I couldn't soothe myself into sleep, I looked over at my nightstand to inspect my unhealthy sleep attachments: a healthy glass of chardonnay, Advil PM, the TV remote, my iPhone at the ready in case something on the ever-present MSNBC set fire to my hair-trigger rage and I needed to post an angry Facebook status. Dr. Ferber would probably suggest that this sleep environment was not ideal for self-soothing. That's the book Dr. Richard Ferber should have written. Someone should have Ferberized me. Let me cry it out, but please come in every five minutes to pat me on the back and let me know, "It's okay. We're here. You're not alone."

Daughter, Divorcée, Storyteller, Jew?

When I first started spending time with my ex-husband's family, the difference between our two clans was a shock to me. His family's favorite pastime was to sit together for hours on end telling and retelling stories of the past and present. Pots of coffee and packs of cigarettes would fuel endless tales of their relatives both alive and dead. Their ideal vacation would be a cluster of cottages situated lakeside so they could wake up and go to sleep in close proximity to one another, starting and ending the day *visiting*, as they called it—regaling each other with stories that had been told so many times they could have sung them in unison. After I had been part of the group for a few years, I had heard the stories enough times that I could have sung along too. The stories were brought out like photo albums. The kids would make requests of some of the old favorites: "Tell about when the cousins snuck out on Fourth of July to light fireworks and set the dock on fire." "Tell us about Uncle Tom and his fighter plane over the Pacific." "Tell us about Grandpa coming to this country and selling hats." "Aunt Frida's candy store." "When Cousin Ralph cooked dinner for Robert Kennedy." "Why did Aunt Mary go bald?" I knew the stories so well I'd sometimes get confused about which ones I'd just heard about as opposed to participated in.

My family was different. Reminiscing wasn't a soothing pastime. If a story got repeated in my house, it was quickly shut down with, "You already told me that." My mother and father held on to their personal history like well-guarded secrets.

When I was growing up and had projects that required background information, like a family tree, for instance, my father would stubbornly refuse to answer any questions about his heritage. When I tell people this, they don't understand. "What do you mean? What does he say when you ask him what nationality he is?"

"He changes the subject," I tell them, leading more than one of my friends to speculate that my father must be hiding something very dark from his past.

My parents simply aren't interested in legends or history or the passing down of family lore. I think that's why I love old things: antiques, houses, and thrift store clothes. My family referred to my vintage wedding gown as the "dead bride dress."

My family is funny. My family is funny in a way that most people would find disturbing. We make jokes where feelings are supposed to be. We're uncomfortable with public displays of affection and sharing. We don't like rituals designed to comfort and bring people together. In other words, we're Scandinavians. We move away from our feelings. Sometimes literally. My sister died at the age of forty-one. I grew up with no customs or traditions to contain the shock and pain of death. A few weeks after my sister's funeral (an observance my parents certainly would have forgone altogether if not for her husband's insistence), my father drove an hour and a half away from our family home—the house that held the memories of my sister—and made an offer on another house, sight unseen by my mother or anyone else. And they moved away from those memories. Problem solved. Forget about the fact that it put them two and a half hours away from their grandkids and me—it was every man for himself now. We don't stew in our feelings. Which is why I suppose I was always so taken with my friends' Jewish families. They seemed like Crock-Pots to me, making warm meals of their traditions and turning their grief into a time when they are surrounded by the potatoes and carrots of their community—warmed by the broths of friendship and healed by the simmering juice of shared memories. Scandinavians are fast food. We drive through our feelings, consume them in our car, and throw them away at the next rest stop on the side of the road—feeling a wave of shame and regret but vowing to be healthier in the future.

I'm not trying to idealize Jews. Or Crock-Pots. I know everything that's cooked in one sort of tastes the same. I know everything gets a little too comfortable and the carrots overstay their welcome. I know. I've dated a lot of Jewish guys. Also, it's not a perfect analogy: Are we the food or the people eating the food? Maybe we're both. The Jewish family is both the comfort food and the family that gathers around the table to eat the meal. My ex-husband's family is Lebanese. Also Crock-Pot people. My many friends in AA are Crock-Pot people too, healed by group sharing as they are. I went to a few Al-Anon meetings in my thirties, and the empathetic looks and warm hugs sent me running to my car at the first smoke break. I've fired more than one therapist for being too compassionate. I need tough love or none at all. I'm not genetically cut out for mush.

Fast-food people rarely say "I'm sorry" or "I love you" unless someone's getting on a plane and we've had a premonition that they might die in a fiery crash, in which case the *I love you* is muttered quickly with embarrassment at the end of a phone call and if someone ever were asked to repeat it, we would definitely say, "Never mind." The Lizer apology goes like this: You get into a fight where dreadful, hurtful things are said—personal, terrible things—the kind of things that make you wonder how you'll ever walk them back. The phone is slammed down without a resolution. A couple of days pass. Angry emails are written but not sent (but saved in the drafts folder because that was a really good line). After four days, you make the phone call, because you're the bigger person.

"Hey, Mom."

"Hey."

"I'm getting rid of that sofa in my family room. Do you have any use for it?"

"Oh. I could use that in the TV room. Are you sure you don't need it?"

"I don't. I'm going to move my desk in there."

"Sure."

"I'll bring it out to you next weekend."

"Thanks. Bye, honey."

Done. The rift is repaired. Never to be spoken of again.

Crock-Pot families can usually be described as *tribal*, the kind of families that have dozens of distant cousins that all gather for family reunions where they make T-shirts to identify themselves as members of the tribe. It's hard to get kicked out of a Crock-Pot tribe. You can get shitfaced drunk, steal a twenty from your nephew's birthday card, and rip Nana's pearls off her neck at Thanksgiving, and you'll still be at the table for the next holiday meal because "you're family." I've been divorced from my ex for sixteen years, and I'm still in with his family. In a fast-food family, you could not pay child support for fourteen years and deal drugs to foster children and still be okay, but you might get banished for forgetting to write a thank-you card for a Christmas gift. The rules are murky and ever-changing. You never really know where you stand in a fast-food family.

As my parents have gotten older, their lips have loosened, and while they haven't started telling stories exactly, they have started dropping bombs.

Occasionally, an odd detail from my family history will slip out, like when I told my parents I was considering getting myself a pet pig and my dad said, "Be careful. My uncle Frank got eaten by a pig."

"What are you talking about, Dad?"

"He lived on a farm and fell into the pigpen when he was feeding them, and they ate him because pigs are omnivorous."

My dad was seventy-five years old and that was the first time I heard that a close relative was eaten by a pig. That was also the first time I'd heard of an uncle Frank.

My dad obviously came by his enigmatic tendencies naturally. When my grandmother on my father's side died, we all found out she had been married before she was married to my grandfather when my parents were going through papers in her attic.

My shock produced a laugh from my parents, which then led to my discovery that my dad had also been married before he was married to my mom. They wed before he went to Korea, and the first Mrs. Lizer still worked as a salesperson in the Crescent department store in Spokane, which is why my mother wouldn't shop there when we visited in the summer. I was thirty years old when I learned this news.

My mother's story is even more mysterious. The tidbits that have been gathered over the years are so sparse and so bizarre I'm not sure if I actually heard them, dreamed them, or am remembering scenes from an Ingmar Bergman movie. My mother is Swedish but was born in Finland. Or the opposite. My mother is a moving target. I feel whichever way I tell her story, she will insist I have it backward. Her mother, Ingeborg, had two sisters. When their mother died, the father remarried a terrible woman, referred to as "the step-monster," who was dreadful to the three girls.

The middle sister couldn't take it anymore, got in a canoe, rowed herself out to the middle of the lake in front of their house in Finland (or Sweden), tied bricks to her ankles, and tossed herself overboard, committing suicide. I only heard this story once from my grandma. When I asked my mother questions about it, she said, "Who told you that?"

I said, "Grandma."

To which she replied, "Oh. I guess so then."

"That's what you have to say about your fifteen-year-old aunt tying bricks to her ankles and throwing herself out of a canoe?" I'm not the crazy one in this story, right? My mother never wanted to tell me too much about her mother because she feared I'd idolize her. Inga had three children by three different men, then kicked all the men to the curb, and I once said when I was in high school I thought that sounded like a good idea. It was hard to get any more information out of her after that.

At the end of her life, my grandmother lived at the Salton Sea, a briny, possibly toxic lake in the California desert, sitting right on top of the San Andreas Fault. It's isolated and desolate, like living on the moon. I'd visit her, and we'd smoke cigarettes in her garage—away from her oxygen tank. We'd play Scrabble without talking much except for her to tell me she didn't think I was attractive enough to be in front of the camera as an actress, but my brain was good, so maybe I could be a director. That was her idea of a compliment. When she died, she was cremated, and my parents went out to the desert and illegally threw her ashes off the side of the road.

Last week I found out that my dad's dad had five siblings. Their parents couldn't afford them and gave all five up to foster care. My grandfather ended up in a foster home with people who beat him on a regular basis, and he ran away at fourteen, living on his own after that. I thought my grandfather was an only child.

"Oh, no," my dad says, his tongue much looser now that Alzheimer's is eating away at the protective barrier that used to keep his secrets. "I've got something like forty-five cousins." What? We have a giant tribe? We could have been having family reunions with T-shirts this whole time.

Finally, one recent Christmas morning, as everyone was having brunch at my house, I tried to slip in the burning question I'd been wanting the answer to for years. Taking advantage of my father's low resistance, I casually asked, "What nationality are you, Dad?"

Without missing a beat, he said, "Jewish." When I reacted, he corrected himself with a hasty "Dutch."

I looked around the table. My mother was eating her quiche, unperturbed. "Did you hear that? Are we Jewish?" Nobody responded.

I know for a fact my mother would deny all of this if you called her up right now. Because that's another thing she does, accuses me of imagining things that really happened. But that's okay. I'm going to run with it. Because I've always done things differently in the family I created. I tell my stories over and over to my kids, whether they want to hear them or not. I say, "I love you." I say, "I'm sorry." Maybe having kids has softened me, and I'm more of a stew than I used to be. Or wanting to tell my stories is a reaction to my parents' refusal to tell their stories. Or maybe I'm not as Scandinavian as I thought I was because suddenly I feel this urge to build a lakeside compound and start and end the day surrounded by my kids. We'll reminisce and play cards, and they'll ask me to tell the one about the time Grandpa said we were Jewish.

We'll Call That Love

The college counselors at my children's high school have asked me to speak next week at their seniors Parent Night. The theme of the event is "Dealing with Transition." They've asked me to participate because I might be able to offer some insight and strategies for coping with the emptying nest. My twins graduated three years ago and sailed off to distant colleges—my daughter in Scotland, my son in Boston. My youngest is still at home, but he's only a year away from making his getaway too. They provided me with a few suggested talking points. The first one was this: How do you stay connected to your children and attend to their needs from so far away? Should I break the bad news to them? You don't.

I was warned when my kids were about to go off that I shouldn't expect to hear much from them if things were going well. It's when there's trouble or unhappiness that you get the phone calls, so consider yourself lucky if you don't speak to them for days on end. Well. No. That wasn't going to work for me. They couldn't just cut me off because they found something better to do, and I extracted promises from both of them that no matter what, they would stay in touch. I offered one hundred extra dollars monthly in the bank account to whichever one called most often—twins respond well to competition. It's fine.

Both kids found themselves instantly enamored with their schools of choice. They made fast friends and loved the freedom of college life, which was great. But what about me? My son was completely awful about staying in touch with me.

Phone calls went unanswered, texts weren't returned, and even though I knew this was supposed to be a good sign, I was frantic. I had to do something.

And this crisis led to strategies designed to force my son to honor *my* feelings of loss over *his* feelings of independence (we'll call that love), which I would now share with the parents of Campbell Hall.

When days would go by without a word from him, I tried to lure him out of his silence with questions left on his voice mail that I didn't really need answers to.

I started light and friendly with things like, "Hi, honey, I'm going to take your car in and get that scrape taken care of. Do you know the approximate date of the accident? I might be able to write it off." No part of that was true, but he would have no way of knowing that since I'm the one who had taken care of all the boring details of his life so far. He'd never filled out an insurance form—a write-off meant nothing to him. And I got nothing back. So I'd try again twenty minutes later, injecting a little fear. "Hi, sweetheart, do you want me to make an appointment for your wisdom teeth during winter break? We really should get that taken care of before you start having pain—those teeth will start growing right into the bone, and you will want to die. Let me know!" When he still didn't respond, I'd try again, slightly less cheerful, more direct: "Hey, bud, Donna's son is thinking about applying to your school. I need to know if I can give him your phone number so he can ask you a few questions. Call me." Still nothing.

I got increasingly less light and definitely more desperate. "Hey, Elias, I'm getting stuff ready to donate to the veterans. If you want to keep any of your soccer gear, you need to let me know by tomorrow. Where are you?" I thought this would get him since he's practically a hoarder—a word he finds offensive, but the guy has held on to every pair of soccer cleats he's worn on every team he's belonged to since the fifth grade.

A couple of years ago, I thought one of the cats was peeing in the house. I bought a black light and was crawling around the floor like a crazy lady trying to find out where the smell was coming from—it led me straight to Elias's room and the "cleat museum." Turns out "old pubescent foot" smells a lot like cat piss. But even my threat of donating his prized possessions didn't get a return phone call or text from my beloved boy, so finally,

I got downright hostile: "Hey. You're obviously busy enjoying the outrageously expensive private college education that I fucking pay for. You're welcome. Too bad I raised a douchebag."

This would usually get a pretty quick phone call that started with him saying, "Mom! I was sleeping. What's the matter with you?"

I would usually say something like, "What? I wasn't serious. God, get a sense of humor."

Him: "What was funny about that? I played it for my friends; they think you're psycho."

Me: "Well, I played it for *my* friends; they think I'm funny." Not true. *My* friends were away at college.

I started to realize that I would have to employ the same strategy that I used to use with my potential high school boyfriends: I had to play it cool. I'd swear that I wasn't going to call him again until he called me first. The problem with giving someone the silent treatment when they are having the time of their life away from you is that they don't notice they're being frozen out.

So then I'd have to call to *inform* him I wasn't going to call, which made me seem super desperate and not all aloof and mysterious like I was going for. God, I was totally blowing this. Very much like I did with my potential high school boyfriends.

When the passive-aggressive and purely aggressive phone calls didn't work and the cold shoulder seemed to make him happy, I realized I had to develop a new strategy to make him dependent on me (we'll call that love), and this is what I would share with the parents of Campbell Hall: If they aren't responding to your texts and emails, call the bank and tell them your credit card has been stolen, the one that he has for "emergencies." The first time he tries to charge his "emergency" burrito at Chipotle and that card gets rejected, you can be sure you'll get a phone call in no time.

When you give up on direct contact and are just looking to stay abreast of their movements and activities, another strategy that is effective but slightly evil requires iPhones connected by a family plan with your service provider. Simply go to the settings menu, text messages, add your child's number to your preferences, and instantly you'll start receiving copies of their texts, ingoing and outgoing, without them knowing. This can be very informative and definitely makes you feel like you're part of their lives once again. In my defense, I discovered this by accident. Our phones got linked through some iCloud glitch. I just didn't look for a way to unlink them right away. Three weeks. It was the only way to make sure he was alive! It's the college equivalent of looking into their crib and making sure they're still breathing.

When the texts started coming to my phone, I felt like I was really in the know, and I liked it. I knew where everyone was meeting after soccer practice. I knew where the parties were this weekend. I knew some unwanted details about what some friend with a New Jersey area code did with a dance major named "Haley" after the party at "Toad's" house. I also knew that it was very, very wrong to invade another person's privacy like that. Even if you gave birth to that person and they're being a dick by not staying in touch even though they know how much that hurts you. It's wrong and can end up biting you in the ass when the text tone wakes you up in the middle of the night and there's a message to your son: "Dude. Did the police just let you go?" There is such a thing as too much knowing.

Which then brings me to Annabel. My daughter has decided she loves Scotland. She uses expressions like *queue up* and tells me that her new *flat* doesn't have a *lift*, so she has to walk the stairs. She refers to some guy in town named Hash as her bartender. She doesn't freeze me out. She tells me everything. When she's at school, she Skypes me sometimes daily. Sometimes drunk. Sometimes hungover. Sometimes when she should be in class. Always in bed. She thinks she's my bud. She laughingly tells me, with the bluster of nineteen, stories of friends who got lost on their way home from a party and were found the next morning sleeping on the beach that they thought was their couch. Or someone who thought they were being kidnapped by a weirdo taxi driver but managed to jump out of the car when he stopped to light his cigarette. It's all adventure to her, and I know that she exaggerates the details to make her seem wilder than she is, the same way I exaggerate my stories to make me seem crazier than I am—but it puts a knot in my stomach. Because I know that in spite of their good fortune and big brains and mostly good sense so far, bad things can happen out there.

I know because Stephanie Cohen, the coolest girl in our group, got lost to heroin addiction. And Mark Wilder, our nineteen-year-old small-time pot dealer, wrapped his car around a tree. And Marie Merrick killed herself over a bad breakup at twenty-two.

And now we're supposed to turn our babies loose in the world and just hope for the best? The unknowing is unacceptable, and the knowing is unbearable. Okay. Maybe I won't share this with the parents of the current graduating class. They'll learn it soon enough on their own. Maybe I'll just skip over that talking point.

The second thing they'd like for me to discuss is this: Since you still have one child at home, how has the family dynamic changed given that two left at once? Right. My poor youngest child, who has become the focus of my laser-like attention (we'll call that love) in the absence of his brother and sister. Because it's just the two of us now, we are able to enjoy a much more intimate relationship since I don't have to divide my attention among three human beings. Things have loosened up around the house. Not wanting to repeat the mistakes of the past—like urging his brother and sister to get as far away from home as possible and experience the world!—I'm slightly less concerned with his SAT scores. Would it be the worst thing to bomb out at your college of choice and spend a couple of years regrouping at our local community college? No, it would not. Think of the fun we'll have! We can eat pancakes for dinner and keep the pool heated all year round. I'm trying to make home the best place there is. We watch TV while we eat; there are no chores or pressure to do something meaningful with his weekends. It's all about keeping my man happy . . . keeping my son happy.

And mostly he's enjoying the extra attention and perks that come with being an only child, though sometimes it's too much and he pretends to have more homework than he actually does just so he can stay in his room and take a break from me. I get it. I'm a lot.

The final topic they'd like for me to discuss is this: What strategies do you recommend for adjusting to your new empty-nest status? Different parents cope with loss differently. I worked through my abandonment issues the only way I know how: I wrote a TV pilot about it.

THE MIDDLE AGES

Pilot

INT. DORM ROOM—MOVE-IN DAY

A small, standard dorm room at a private East Coast college. Zach, eighteen and unsure, and his dad, Brad, fifty-one and good-natured, stand helplessly off to the side while a mani-cally upbeat Amy, Zach's mother, Brad's wife, is sucking the air from a space bag with a hand pump.

Zach's dorm room has been organized and color coor-dinated within an inch of its life. There are perfectly con-trasting linens, a pop-up hamper, desk caddy, mini-fridge, laundry drying rack, iPhone charger/speaker, etc. It's an ad for the Bed Bath & Beyond college catalog.

AMY

(AS SHE PUMPS) You're going to want to swap out your summer clothes for the winter ones around October. I've got Boston weather on my phone, so I'll text you. Then you just put it all in these bags, suck out the air, pop it in the under-bed bin, and ta-da, no storage problem!

Amy seals the collapsed space bag, places it in the under-bed storage container, rolls it under the bed, and looks around.

AMY (CONT'D)

There you go! All the comforts of home!

REVEAL ZACH'S ROOMMATE, sitting on his bare mat-tress on the other, undecorated side of the room. His par-ents are nowhere in sight. He's staring at Amy's masterpiece and clutching an Xbox.

Amy crosses to Zach, holding a large framed picture of the two of them.

AMY (CONT'D)

(RE: THE PICTURE) Um, I don't know where you want to put this, sweetie. There's not much more room on the desk, but maybe you can use some of that sticky putty I put in your desk drawer to hang it on the wall. It doesn't damage the paint.

ZACH

It's kind of big.

AMY

Oh, I get it. You don't want a big picture of your mom in your dorm room?

She laughs, as if she's a good sport, then snatches the picture away.

BRAD

Okay. Well, I guess we'll leave you to it, buddy. (SEARCHING FOR PARENTAL WISDOM) Drink responsibly.

Amy looks at Brad as if to say, "Seriously?"

ZACH

Okay, Dad. Bye. Bye, Mom.

AMY

Bye? Eighteen years and then just bye?

Amy looks to Brad and realizes that's exactly right.

AMY (CONT'D)

Right. Well. Bye.

There's a moment where nobody moves. Brad breaks it by hugging Zach.

BRAD

I'm proud of you, Z.

ZACH

Thanks, Dad.

Zach turns to Amy.

ZACH (CONT'D)

Thanks, Mom.

AMY

I didn't do anything.

Amy quickly hugs Zach, then pulls away with a crisp pat on his shoulder.

AMY (CONT'D)

You're going to be great!

ZACH

I love you, Mom.

AMY

Yep. Yep.

With that, Amy, picture in hand, turns and walks out the door, a frozen smile on her face. Brad follows.

EXT. DORM—MOMENTS LATER

Brad and Amy come out of the building into the September sunshine. Amy still has the smile on her face.

BRAD

Oh shit. I forgot to give Zachy a credit card. I'll be right back.

Amy nods, smile still frozen. Brad exits back inside. A beat, then Amy drops to the ground like a stone. She clutches the photo and starts to cry. Quiet and contained, at first, then progressively louder and messier. The crying gains momentum until she's crying so hard it looks like she might hurt herself. Other parents and students stop to watch, unsure of what to do.

After a few moments of this, Brad comes back out and discovers her, wailing like a wounded animal on the ground.

BRAD (CONT'D)

Honey?

He quickly crosses to her.

BRAD (CONT'D)

Honey? Amy? What happened? Did you fall down?

AMY

(SCREAMING) I did everything for that fucking ingrate, and now he's leaving me! He'll die without me! (SOBBING HARDER) I'll die without him.

Brad crouches down to her, wildly embarrassed by the scene.

BRAD

(WEAKLY) He's coming home for Thanksgiving. (THEN) Let's get you up.

Amy makes no move to get up or stop crying. Brad desperately tries to get her to her feet. He grabs Amy under her arms and tries to lift. She's limp and uncooperative. He tries to go at it from another angle, attempting to scoop her up, but he can't get a handle on her limbs. It's a mess.

INT. RENTAL CAR—A SHORT TIME LATER

Brad and Amy have made it to their rental car in the dorm parking lot. Brad sits in the driver's seat, Amy next to him, staring blindly ahead, drinking beer out of a can. The crying has subsided, but every once in a while, a little hiccup/sob escapes.

BRAD

That was nice of that kid to give you a beer.

AMY

I'm done, Brad. Nobody needs me anymore. I wish I belonged to that tribe that takes their old women and leaves them on rocks to die.

BRAD

What?

AMY

Yeah. I read it in a book.

BRAD

By book you mean Huffington Post?

AMY

When the women can't have babies anymore and their bones get too brittle to carry firewood, they set them out on rocks and leave them to die.

BRAD

Where?

AMY

On rocks.

BRAD

Where are the rocks?

AMY

I don't remember.

BRAD

But not in America?

AMY

I don't know.

BRAD

You're saying this is happening currently or a long time ago?

AMY

I don't know.

BRAD

Why can't you ever finish an article? They're like two paragraphs long.

AMY

(HOPELESS) I don't know.

Brad reaches out and carefully touches Amy's shoulder.

> **BRAD**
>
> *We're going to get through this.*

Amy looks at him for a beat as if she doesn't know how to break it to him.

> **AMY**
>
> *You know, Brad, no offense, but we're not going through it. It's different for me.*

> **BRAD**
>
> *How, Amy? How is it different for you?*

> **AMY**
>
> *You have a job. Zach was my job.*

> **BRAD**
>
> *Yeah, I have a job. I'm a publishing rep, trying to sell books to bookstores. Guess what doesn't exist anymore. Books. And bookstores. It's like trying to sell record players to dinosaurs.*

> **AMY**
>
> *(COMPLETELY IGNORING HIM) I did every god-damn thing for that kid. He's average. At best. And I pushed his below-average ass like a boulder up a hill for eighteen years. I was room parent and team*

46

mom and orthodontist appointment maker and barf cleaner-upper, and what do I get?

BRAD

You get a great kid who's healthy and happy and going to college.

AMY

Big deal.

BRAD

What do you want?

AMY

A little goddamn acknowledgment that I sacrificed the best years of my life so that he can repay me by leaving me in the dust.

BRAD

He appreciates you.

AMY

No. He doesn't. He barely tolerates me. He couldn't wait to get away from me. In fact, if you and I were trapped in a burning building and he could only save one of us, guess who it would be.

BRAD

(HAPPY) Me?

AMY

*That's right. Mr. "See you when I see you" fun
parent, "drink responsibly" dad. He's an ungrateful,
spoiled brat.*

BRAD

Then why are you going to miss him?

AMY

Because he's my soul mate!

That hangs in the air between them. Amy offers Brad a sip
of her beer. He takes it.

END OF ACT ONE

The thirty-year-old HBO executive didn't get it. He said, "Why
is the mom so upset? The kid's eighteen. Of course he's leaving
home. Can she really be surprised?"

To which I replied, "Ask your mother."

The answer, Campbell Hall parents of the class of 2017, is
yes. It's a surprise. Even though everything you have done up
until this point is in preparation for their eventual departure—
the tutors, the college tours, the nagging, the tears, the speech
therapists, the educational therapists, the marriage counselors, the extracurricular activities that will look good on an

application, the community service, the threats, the bribes, the struggle—all leading to this moment. And still, I thought they were bluffing. So the only wisdom I can offer is this: try so hard to be happy that they're happy, even when it makes you sad. We'll call *that* love.

Empty Nest

In the past two weeks, several people have asked if I'm okay.

"Why?" I ask.

"Well, you're talking about your chickens a lot. You're kind of obsessed with them. Doing all right with the twins off at school?"

"What? Yes. Of course. I'm fine. Just a little trouble at the house."

My twins had left for college. And, yes, when two of your three children leave at once, it's a bit of a shock, but I was dealing with an actual crisis at home, a chicken crisis. The safety of my backyard flock had been threatened. Even so, I wouldn't say I was obsessed. I just had to handle it. A hawk had suddenly discovered my free-ranging ladies and came swooping down one day, sinking his talons into poor Hen Solo's feathered backside. Fortunately, Hen Solo is a hefty girl, and the hawk couldn't lift her more than a few inches before she dropped back to the ground with only flesh wounds, but the girls were freaked.

Especially Princess Layer and Chew Bak Bak, who immediately stopped laying eggs and took to hiding under the bushes during daylight hours, clucking in worry. The chickens count on me to protect them. I've looked out for them every day of their lives from the first day they hatched, and I wasn't going to stop now when they really needed me. Something had to be done.

I did a little internet research and learned that once hawks have discovered your flock, it is nearly impossible to dissuade them from attacking again, and there are very few ways of handling the problem other than locking away your hens in a predator-proof enclosure.

My chickens had lived carefree in my backyard their whole lives, and it pained me to think of caging them up, but birds of prey are federally protected, so even throwing a rock at that nasty hawk was a $12,000 fine. Not that I would harm even an evil bully bird anyway . . . but this is where I started getting a little consumed, maybe. I was determined that my hens would remain free. So first I built a scarecrow. Unfortunately, there was nothing scary about her. She was wearing my overalls from high school, a nice linen tunic shirt from the Sundance catalog, gardening gloves, and a sunbonnet. I spent more time putting her outfit together than I did dressing myself in the morning. She looked like Diane Lane in *Under the Tuscan Sun*. The hawk planted himself in my pine tree to watch my nonsense. My scarecrow did nothing to shake his confidence. Next I bought a fake owl and falcon. I read that in order to make this deterrent effective, you had to move them around the yard so the hawk is fooled into thinking they're real competitors because hawks don't like competition. Who does? I went out a dozen times a day and moved the fake birds to different locations, making what I thought were very convincing owl and falcon noises in the process. I put them on trees and in fences. I even climbed up a ladder and put the fake falcon on the roof. When I climbed down the ladder, I looked out at the yard and saw the hawk, in the pine tree, still watching me. He flew out of the tree and did a low flyover over the pool—a total dick move, as if to say, "This is what a real bird looks like, asshole."

After a week, the hawk got even more brazen. He would be waiting in the walnut tree next to the coop when I went out in the morning to turn the girls out into the yard.

He wasn't giving up, and I didn't see any way out of it: for their own safety, I was going to have to lock up the chickens. So I called Paco.

Paco had done a few small carpentry jobs for me around the house and had always impressed me with his skill and neatness. I asked if he thought he could handle a chicken enclosure. He said he could. I hated that my girls were going in a cage. I hated that my beautiful backyard was going to have a big chicken jail plopped right in the middle of it. The hawk had ruined everything. I didn't entirely trust Paco's aesthetic sensibilities, so I spent a long time overexplaining how much my backyard meant to me and how depressed I would be if the chicken enclosure was some big, ugly thing ruining my bucolic retreat I so carefully cultivated, that it was really the only thing that made city living tolerable for me. I showed Paco pictures of charming and attractive coops culled from Pinterest to drive the point home that I really needed this coop to be cute. About halfway through my explanation of how seriously awful this would be for me if we couldn't get this right, I realized how shallow I must sound to Paco: the obnoxious white lady bumming that her organically fed poultry wouldn't be able to lounge by the pool anymore while he probably has to worry about ICE breaking down his door to take Uncle Francisco back to Mexico for a traffic ticket he got in 1994. Shit. I wanted Paco to understand that I'm *not* the obnoxious white lady. I hate white people too! But I'm having a hard time. My kids have gone away, the hawk has ruined the tranquility in my backyard, and I just need a cute coop. Now Paco thinks I'm an asshole. I hate the hawk.

When Paco presented me with his design for the chicken enclosure, I was stunned. His drawing was detailed and professional, perfectly to scale.

He had incorporated everything I'd babbled to him into the design and presented me with a perfectly drawn chicken dream house—as good as any I'd seen from an architect. Paco was going to make everything okay. Did I mention that Paco was handsome?

Once he started building, it only got better. He revealed himself to be a true artisan. The angles of the pergola that would be the outdoor living space echoed the angles of the persimmon tree it perfectly lined up next to. The coop itself was situated on the property in such a way that it looked as if it had been part of the original concept. Not a chicken man himself, Paco nonetheless considered the chickens' needs when he designed the ramp that led to their coop, understanding that when the girls are heavy with eggs, a long uphill climb can be uncomfortable, so having the nesting boxes just inside the door with the easiest access possible is best. When thinking about the seasons, he gave the ladies several eaves under which to find shelter from rain or intense sun. He thought it would be more aesthetically pleasing if the coop mirrored the architectural design of the main house, like a guesthouse, so he trimmed the windows and framed the doors in the same style and matching paint. Paco was building me a masterpiece. A chicken mansion that not only kept my girls safe but made me want to spend even more time in my backyard than before. You know why? Because Paco cared about me. He listened to me. He understood my needs. I was in love with Paco. But Paco could never love me because I wasn't good enough for him. How could Paco ever respect me? I get paid money to write jokes. I can't actually do anything.

I can't draw anything. I can't build anything. I can't even work outside because my hormone replacement cream makes me overly sensitive to the sun. Paco must think I'm worthless.

The impossibility of our love became even more apparent when the gardeners and my dog walker, Elizabeth, gathered around to admire the chicken mansion and say in all seriousness, "That is much nicer than my apartment." I said it too. Just because I wanted to fit in, but for me it wasn't true. My house is still nicer than the chicken coop.

Paco worked fast, faster than I wanted him to, and by the end of the week, he was nearly done. On Saturday afternoon, I had to go to a fancy friend's house for a play reading. I promised I would come, but I really didn't want to leave my backyard and Paco because I could tell our time was growing short. I loved my friend, and she loved me, but I was so much more comfortable talking chickens and tacos with Paco than standing in Santa Monica in my friend's perfect house, trying to figure out how I was supposed to attack this buffet with its mini kale salads in mini glass cups with mini silver spoons, and hold on to my wineglass so the overzealous busperson wouldn't sweep it away while at the same time balancing a compostable bamboo cheese plate—I would have to have five hands. Whenever someone asked what was going on with me, I would, of course, tell them about the chicken mansion. They'd laugh, realize I wasn't kidding, then drift away, leaving me to balance my kale cup, wine, and cheese alone. I didn't belong in this world. I belonged with Paco. If I spoke better Spanish, I would have told him, "I'm not what I seem, Paco. I am much more like you than I am like me."

But I knew that if it sounded that bad in English, it probably really wouldn't come off well in my broken Spanish. When I got back home, Paco was gone, but he'd left me a note—well, not a note, a bill.

The chicken mansion was done, and so was my time with Paco.

All of the chickens were really happy except for Teri Hatcher, which was not surprising. She'd been disgruntled since the day she was laid. The first couple of days, I kept a list in the kitchen of things I was going to call Paco to come back and fix. Teensy little complaints, excuses to bring him back to me: he left the latch off one of the gates, the stickers on the windows, a couple of his paint buckets in the garage . . . all things I could easily handle myself, but I didn't want to. I wanted Paco to do them because Paco would do them perfectly.

The last time I saw Paco, he came back to get paid. He wasn't wearing his work clothes. He had on khakis and a button-down shirt. He looked beautiful. I told him I loved the chicken mansion so much I couldn't even stand it. I was going to take pictures of it and make him a photo album. I told him he could definitely get a lot of work in places like the Palisades making coops for obnoxious rich white ladies who fancied themselves urban chicken farmers—not real ones like me. We laughed; it was bittersweet. I told him I'd hook him up. I'd be his agent.

He told me, "You work too hard."

I said, "Me? I don't do anything. You're the one."

Then he said, "You're a good mom."

I said, "How do you know? My kids are all gone."

He said he could tell by the way I took care of my chickens. I, of course, burst into tears. That would have been the perfect time for Paco to kiss me. He didn't. He looked super embarrassed. I think he was going to church with his wife. I gave him his check, then went into the house, where my dog walker, Elizabeth, hugged me because she's used to me. And there was no one else to do it.

When it was getting dark, I was closing up the chickens for the night and wondering if I was actually losing my mind. Paco. The chickens. My empty nest.

Of course, it all makes a certain amount of sense that I feel this intense attachment to my chicks right now. There's nothing I wouldn't do to protect them. And the other ones are so far away, and I can't keep them safe from the hawks.

Denial

My parents have lost two of their four children, and I like to say, "One more to go, and I'll be the favorite." Saying things like that is the reason I'm so unpopular in my own family. Truth is not appreciatcd. My parents live in a state of denial, in the neighborhood of unfelt feelings, on a dead-end street of cheap scotch and jug Chablis. They don't want to stop tanning, so skin cancer is a myth. They have a "system" in Vegas. And a drinking hiatus is not an option, so they just refuse to read the drug interaction warnings on their ever-increasing bottles of medications, and why do I have to be such a downer?

My brother died of heart failure due to chronic methamphetamine abuse. My mother and father prefer that he died of a tragic and rare *genetic* heart irregularity even though it sent my freaked-out niece running to her doctor to be tested for a heart condition made up by my mom and dad. When my sister was dying of a brain tumor and was in hospice, my mother wouldn't admit that she was unresponsive. She said *they* talked all the time, and if Lisa wasn't speaking to me when I sat with her, it was probably because of something I did, and I better search my conscience to figure out what it was. And the Thanksgiving immediately following my divorce, when my ex-husband had my kids for the holiday; my only remaining sibling was at his in-laws' family; and the three of us, my mother, my father, and I, sat around the Thanksgiving table, the lone survivors of our decimated family, forks clinking noisily, my mother loudly declared: "Well, I think this is the best Thanksgiving ever!"

My dad agreed. "More leftovers for us!"

Their belief in their delusions is so unflinching that when they insist a couch is a car, you think *you* must be the crazy one.

The truth is, they don't want the truth. They like the lie. I have spent much of my life trying to get them to face reality, get their feet on the ground, heads in the game, their minds on planet Earth. And it's nearly driven me crazy, until recently when I've finally begun to understand them because a light bulb went out in my kitchen.

There are three recessed lights above the island where the ceiling is twelve feet high. In order to reach a bulb and change it, a six-foot ladder must be placed on top of the four-foot counter. I first have to climb onto the counter, then climb to the very top step on the ladder, and then stretch to my full height to reach the bulb and unscrew it, balancing myself on the swinging pot rack that holds hundreds of pounds of cookware. It's like Cirque du Soleil, but not sexy, just dangerous. If anyone saw me do it, they would definitely tell me not to, but there is no other way to accomplish this task, so I'm doing it anyway. And somehow, against all odds, I get the dead bulb out of the socket and descend the ladder without killing myself.

I went to the hardware store, bulb in hand, and stood in front of the enormous selection of light bulbs for several minutes until finally a helpful, small, gray-haired woman who I later realized was a man—both of us at the cruel age where men's features soften and women grow mustaches—asked if I had any questions about light bulbs.

I told her, "I'm looking to replace something over my kitchen island. It's very high up and hard to get to, but I need good light because it's where I cut things with sharp knives and bad eyesight."

She started asking questions: "Do you prefer flood or spot?"

Me: "Flood."

She: "Natural daylight or soft light?"

Me (excited because I didn't know that was an option): "Ooh, natural daylight."

Him (because this is where I realized she was a man): "Incandescent? CFL? LED?"

I was stumped.

He explained, "Incandescent are the old-fashioned bulbs. Regular life-span. Maybe last you a year and a half of regular

60

use. CFLs are next. Energy efficient. Could last five years. But if I were you, I'd go for the LED. They're pricey. About twenty bucks. But with moderate use, an LED's going to last you something in the range of thirty years. You'll pay more now, but you may never have to change that light bulb again."

He picked up an LED from the rack in front of us, handed it to me, and walked away. I stared at it, and sure enough, right there on the package it promised twenty-five thousand hours of light.

I've never been one of those people who are obsessed with age. I've never taken to my bed, dreading the run-up to a milestone birthday like some people I've known—not at thirty or forty or even fifty. It didn't mean anything to me. I didn't fret about wrinkles or sags. I didn't base my worth on my looks or my youth, so the loss of those things wasn't devastating. Good looks were never my commodity. I had wit and brains and rage. But in the past few years, I had acquired this new habit of marking time by expiration dates. In the grocery store, I'd check the date on my lactose-free half-and-half. "April 15, 2014. Wow. By the time this half-and-half turns, the kids and I will be back from our spring break camping trip. Oh. That's so fast. I can't believe it's over!" But we hadn't even left yet. It was just the idea that that was how quickly things were moving—our vacation would be a memory before the half-and-half went bad. It was a way I had of orienting myself, clocking where I would be in life when the milk goes sour. Orange juice, if it was pasteurized, lasted a little longer. So the news was better. It would get me into summer. "June 25, 2016. School will be out. We'll be in Vermont when the OJ rots." That was a happy thought!

So when the man in the hardware store presented me with light bulbs that would not burn out for thirty years, I stood paralyzed in the aisle, contemplating what this meant for me. When this light bulb burns out, my father will be dead. My mother will be dead. A few less obvious people will be dead too—people who will die prematurely. People who would go to the doctor for yearly checkups and discover advanced pancreatic cancer that they thought was constipation from their vitamins. Maybe even me. If I do survive, I'll be eighty-three years old. Maybe, like the hardware guy, I'll have settled into some kind of gender neutrality and I'll have to wear a pink bow in my thinning gray wisps to clue people into the proper pronoun. If I still give a shit what people think. And people are still using pronouns. My twins will be forty-nine; my youngest will be forty-seven. They'll be married or not. Divorced or not. Have children or not. This will all be decided by then. It won't be a world of possibility like it is for them now at nineteen and seventeen years old. It will be a done deal. They will either feel like life made good on its early promises or let down by it. If I still own the house where this light bulb burns, it will definitely not be advisable for me to get on a ladder on top of the counter and change it myself. If my children are still speaking to me, they might worry about me living alone with lights burning out and think it's time for me to come live with them. But I won't go. I don't think I'll get along with their spouses. Also, if it's up to my children to decide what becomes of me, I could be in trouble.

I'm remembering the dinner when I told my three kids that Vermont had just passed a Death with Dignity law, giving people the right to make their own decisions about end-of-life care. I told them, "Once again, our adopted state of Vermont shows how civilized they are. Isn't that great?"

My children thought for a minute; then Annabel said, "Does that mean we can poison you?"

Elias perked up. "No! Let's feed her to sharks."

Then, Dayton, my baby, finished it off with, "You guys, let's strap antlers to her head and hunt her in the woods!"

Maybe I should have married again. Would it be less lonely with another old person next to me with a blue bow taped to his scalp? But then what if I really loved him and he died first? And now I'm all alone again. Except for my dogs. But wait—my dogs would have died at least twenty years ago. I had to bite the inside of my cheek so I wouldn't lose it right there in the light bulb aisle. And then the little old man/woman would have to come scoop me up off the floor. Maybe I could marry him. But no. He would definitely die first. He looks like he smokes. I'd probably be a widow by the time I was seventy. I have to stop!

I don't want to think about this. I just want a pleasing light shining down on the island in my kitchen when I cook dinner tonight. That's as much as I want to think about.

That's when I suddenly understood why my mother declared it the best Thanksgiving ever. All she wanted to think about in that moment was the fact that the turkey was cooked all the way through and the gravy wasn't lumpy. She wanted to focus on the food sitting on the table, not the people who were no longer sitting at the table. There is such a thing as *too much* reality. I put down the thirty-year LED mindfuck light bulb and picked up a regular GE soft white. Life expectancy: one and a half years.

At which point, my youngest child would be graduated from high school. The twins would be of legal drinking age. I would be fifty-five years old, but my beautiful golden retriever would probably still be alive, if I could keep his weight down. My dad's Alzheimer's symptoms would no doubt be more pronounced, but he would probably still recognize me. And I for sure would still make it up the ladder to change the bulb all by myself, if I could keep *my* weight down. That was enough reality for me.

Sometimes it does us no good at all to think about things that are too hard to think about. That's what poetry is for and music and sex and Mediterranean Mint gelato in my freezer and dogs in my bed. And for my mother and my father and their bigger, harder, more horrible truths—Chablis and scotch and lies.

Winter Break (Down)

It was winter break, and all three kids were going to be sleeping under my roof for the first time in three months. I was counting the minutes until our happy unit would be together again, and I couldn't wait to wow them with my home-cooked meals, hold spontaneous dance parties in the living room, and surprise them with morning movie dates and popcorn and Diet Coke breakfasts. Ten glorious days of family fun time. The house would be alive with noise and activity and love, just like the good old days, but most of all, I would be so busy cooking and cleaning and nurturing that I wouldn't have time to do anything else. And that's exactly what I needed: a giant, exhausting distraction from my state of mind. It had been a grumpy and anxious few weeks. I felt disgruntled and bored but disinterested in all of my options. I think I was in the middle of an existential ennui—though I wasn't exactly sure what that was because part of my condition was lack of ambition, so I didn't bother to look it up.

This is usually when I acquired a new pet, but my household was at maximum capacity. I could tell by a first-time visitor's reaction to my home. I followed their eyes from the three barking dogs to the four cats lounging on every surface to the sign on Annabel's room that read, "Shut the door, loose bunny," until they would finally turn their head toward the sound of a hen passing a large egg from somewhere beyond the pool. They would usually say something like, "I didn't know you had so many animals."

What they meant was, "I didn't know you were an animal-hoarding freak."

So even though I recently heard that hedgehogs make really cute pets, I was going to resist. I just needed a project, I told myself. And my three adult babies home for ten straight days gave me just the distraction I was looking for.

I spent a week preparing for their arrival. Their rooms were perfect, flowers from the garden were placed on their dressers, and their favorite toiletries were stocked to their very specific needs. I knew their allergies, scents, hair challenges, and skin types, and it was all waiting for them—impeccably arranged as if they'd checked into a B&B run by their stalker.

When the day finally arrived, I was skipping through the supermarket aisles, tossing their favorite foods into my shopping cart like a 1950s newlywed expecting her husband home for a romantic dinner. Elias loves Top Ramen and pita chips. For Annabel, those dried seaweed sheets and a bag of Jelly Bellys. A giant box of clementines and organic string cheese for dear Dayton. And finally, individual Nutella packets with pretzel sticks for all three, lovingly placed on their pillows. I spent more than $200 at the market and forgot paper towels, laundry soap, and coffee.

Dayton's vacation had already started, and Elias flew in from Boston the day before. Elias had positioned himself in front of the TV, watching back-to-back international soccer matches. Dayton was on his computer, playing video games, and the last one to come home was Annabel. I hadn't seen her since August, and I missed her so much I was mad at her. She had stopped in Texas to visit with a friend's family on her way home from school in Scotland, so I didn't get her until two days before Christmas. I told the boys I was leaving to pick her up, and when I got back, they better be ready for winter break fun! I'm pretty sure they heard me.

I drove to LAX from Sherman Oaks at 5:00 p.m. on December 23. It took two hours and fifteen minutes to get there. When I told the checker at the market I was making an airport run, she said I should have Annie take a taxi. But I could never do it because I'm pathologically maternal. How could I be the world's greatest mother if I sent a stranger in a taxi to pick up my girl?

"God, I love Houston!" she declared first thing when I saw her in baggage claim, which did not make me happy.

"Welcome home," I prompted.

"Did you even notice my cowboy boots?" she said, ignoring me. Then she tried to kill me: "I think I could totally live in Texas after college."

"I'm not a fan," I pouted.

"Have you ever even been there?" she asked, as if I were some rube who had never left Sherman Oaks.

"Yes. I have. With you. We got stuck there for two days on the way back from the Galapagos. Remember?"

Annabel: "Really? I don't remember that. My childhood's a little hazy."

That's not quite true. Spectacular family vacations might be hazy, but the one time the tooth fairy fell asleep and forgot to leave a dollar under her pillow is crystal clear.

Annabel will insist, "Of course I remember that. It was traumatic."

"It was not traumatic," I tell her. "I covered it really well." Annabel insists I didn't.

Leaving a note and ten bucks the night *after* a person's tooth falls out with the explanation "Tooth Fairy apologizes for the delay. Tooth Fairy, like your mom, is all alone, and no one helps her with anything ever, so maybe you should just give Tooth

Fairy a break" is not the kind of thing that keeps a child's fantasy life flourishing, according to her.

On the three-hour-and-fifteen-minute drive back to Sherman Oaks from the airport, I heard all about her friend's fantastic family. Apparently, the father is really funny. The mother is an amaaaa-zing cook. And so nice. She's always in a good mood.

"No one is always in a good mood, Annabel."

"Rachel is," she insisted.

"That's fucking impossible!" I practically shouted, a case in point.

Annabel said, "You seem angry."

I said I'd been on the freeway for close to four hours. She tells me I should have let her take a taxi. I tell her I wanted to pick her up myself because I'm her mom and I missed her and I thought it would be great of me, even though it was really exhausting and her flight came in at the worst possible time two days before Christmas—but I did it anyway because I'm great. Which, of course, ruined the greatness of it. Which is exactly what my mom does. She talks about anything nice or generous she might do so much that it completely negates anything that might have been nice or generous about it in the first place. I blame Texas for turning me into my mother.

"Are your friend's parents Republicans?" I ask because I can't help myself.

Annabel reacts badly. "Are you still doing that? Judging people by one narrow definition as if that tells you all you need to know about them?"

"Yes," I tell her, wondering when that started being a bad thing.

She tells me it's childish and judgmental. And that it actually makes me a bigot.

The wonderful thing about sending your children off into the world is that when they come back, after meeting all sorts of cool and interesting people, they are able to serve as sort of a mirror. Not a flattering mirror, like the one at the end of the long hallway in the center of my house. The one that makes me look taller than I am and leaner than I am and prettier than I am. They reflect back in a different kind of way. The way that makes me look bad compared with everyone else in the world. Shit. I'd waited so long to see her; why was I picking fights? I had to find a way to get this homecoming back on track.

Back at the house, Elias was watching yet another Spanish soccer match, and Dayton was still playing video games. "Okay! Time to start our beautiful family together time!" I shouted, trying to sound "up" but instead sounding slightly hysterical, like I was calling someone away from the edge of a cliff. It was so late, and I had a headache that made it impossible to open my eyes all the way, but I was determined to salvage my reputation. I cooked like a fiend—quickly marinating chicken breasts in Italian dressing, tossing them on the grill while I threw together an arugula salad with goat cheese, toasted almonds, and raspberries. I whisked balsamic vinaigrette, broiled some asparagus with sea salt and a squeeze of lemon juice and olive oil. Then I announced, "Vacation rules!" We would eat in front of the TV! Annabel protested the soccer game. Dayton wanted to know why they got to pick shows when he got home first. Elias complained that he was halfway through the game, and why did they get to come in and change the channel? My homecoming dinner turned into a squabbling, sniping brawl, ending with all three storming into their rooms, slamming doors, and me, throwing a tantrum, throwing away dinner, washing the dishes, cursing Texas, Christmas, and Republicans—which is pretty much the same thing I do every night when I'm alone.

The next morning, the day before Christmas, I woke up and decided to chalk up the night before to everyone's exhaustion and excitement over being together. Determined to make this the best Christmas Eve ever, I burst into each of the kids' rooms with Fred, our miniature dachshund, under my arm and sang the wake-up song from their childhood: "It's your wiener wake-up call; we're going to wake them all, and if they don't get up, they'll get licked by this pup." I informed them we were all going on a hike in the canyon, just like we used to do on the Christmas Eve mornings when they were little. To say I was not met with enthusiasm is a serious understatement, but I forced them to get out of bed, throw on some clothes, and join me in what I guaranteed would be a great way to start the day.

The beginning of the hike was a wordless trudge with me babbling to fill the silence, reminiscing about hikes of Christmas past: once when it was hotter and one time I remembered it being colder. "But not as cold as today. Today is cold. Brr. Nobody thinks it gets cold in Los Angeles, but it does," I prattled on because I am the only one making conversation until about halfway up the mountain, when it seems their brains and bodies finally woke up and the three of them decided to run the rest of the way up the steep hill. I started to go with them, but soon, I fell behind, winded and whining, "Wait up!" while they disappeared out of sight. When I finally caught up to them at the top, they were barely breathing heavy. I was red-faced, sweaty, and panting, possibly dying. I told them I was just getting over a cold; otherwise, I would have run up too. It would have been no problem. "I've been boxing at the gym," I say between gasps for air.

This, at last, brought a smile to their wicked faces, and they started taking turns with the old lady jokes . . . inquiring about my arthritis, offering to carry me, asking if "Mother" needs a rest. There was a small wooden bench under a tree, and the kids asked if I wanted to sit. "I don't need to sit," I snapped. Then I sat. I really was just getting over a cold.

I noticed a dedication on the bench, and I read it out loud in an effort to change the subject. "'In memory of Sandy McCall. She was always there for you.' Oh. That's nice," I say.

"We'll get you a bench when you go," Annabel tells me. "It will say, 'In memory of Kari Lizer: It's so cold.'"

"Why?"

"Because that's all you ever say," says Annabel.

I tried to defend myself. "That's not true. I said it this morning because it was cold."

"You said it a few times this morning," Elias reminds me.

"She also said it yesterday," Dayton chimes in. "And I'm pretty sure you'll say it tomorrow."

"I might. It's supposed to be cold tomorrow!"

"That's why we're getting you a bench!" All three kids laugh.

Oh great. *Now* they're getting along. And I'm the odd man out. How did this happen? I used to be the funny one. I'm a professional comedy writer! Oh God. Now I really am my mother.

Whenever we used to make fun of her, she would tell us how she was on the ski team at BU and skied Stowe. No matter what we were making fun of her about.

It could be her driving, her cooking, her lack of ability to use a telephone . . . somehow her response was always, "I skied Stowe!"

And now here I am, a prickly, humorless woman, shivering on a bench, the butt of everyone's joke, insisting I'm a comedy writer while nobody laughs.

Back at the house, I locked myself in my room and decided to give up on the forced family fun time. If they wanted to sleep until noon and park themselves in front of the TV, it was fine with me. I had to stop springing out of bed asking who was up for a hike or maybe a movie marathon at the Arclight. "Popcorn and Diet Coke for breakfast, anyone?" No one was buying that I was the fun mom. Apparently, no one ever had. And that was fine. I could occupy myself very nicely on this winter break. I didn't need them. Even so, when they walked into my bedroom that afternoon and found me watching myself acting in an old episode of *Quantum Leap*, it was a new low.

"Oh God, Mom. Is this what you do?" Annabel said, all of them looking at me as if they'd found me with my pants around my ankles.

"No!" I protested. "This isn't what I do. It was just on, and I stopped to watch for a second because I wasn't sure if this was the episode I was in."

Elias took the remote from me, and like Columbo, who had solved the crime but wasn't all that happy about revealing the perpetrator, he pointed the remote at the TV and revealed that I was watching a recording.

"Fine," I said. "I set a search on the DVR with my name to record everything I've ever been in." Elias set the remote back on my bed like he'd accidentally picked up my vibrator. "So what? I can watch myself. I was a good actress! I was in *Matlock*! Andy Griffith thought I was very talented. He loved me!" Suddenly I was fucking Norma Desmond. It was *Sunset Boulevard* in my bedroom. The kids walked out and shut the door softly behind them, my shame complete.

Later, the dinner was quiet. Of course I still made dinner because I'm pathologically maternal. The kids gave each other looks across the table like they were afraid to set me off.

Dayton spoke first. "Mom. We're sorry. We were just joking on the hike. We didn't mean to hurt your feelings. If you didn't have a cold, you probably would have beaten us up that hill. We'll go to the movies with you if you want to."

Elias chimed in next. "I actually heard *Creed* was good. It's about a boxer, like you. Want to go see that?"

Then Annabel: "We could go tonight, but if it's too late, we could go in the morning and have popcorn and Diet Coke breakfast. You love that."

It was 5:30 p.m. But she was right; it was too late. I would never make it.

"I'm not crazy," I told them. Which is what crazy people say. "It's just . . . I got some bad news a couple weeks ago, and I guess it hit me harder than I thought. I think I was putting too much pressure on our winter break to make me feel better. But it's not your job to make me feel better."

They stopped eating and stared at me. Dayton wanted to know what the bad news was. I could tell I was scaring them, so I decided to tell them. "I sent away for my DNA profile. You know those commercials for 23andMe? You spit into a vial for about five minutes—which, by the way, is so much harder than you think it's going to be. You know how I couldn't run up the hill today? I had to rest three times spitting into a vial for five minutes. Anyway, once you get the spit collected, you send it off to these scientists, and they send you back a link to your DNA profile results that tell you all these interesting things about yourself. And, well, I got mine back a few weeks ago."

They nervously waited for me to go on. "Most of it was stuff you could tell from looking in a mirror: sixty-six percent Scandinavian, freckles, blue eyes, light skin. But my muscle profile was really upsetting. It just said, 'Not a sprinter.'"

They stared back at me, trying so hard to be on board. They really are nice people.

Finally, Dayton said, gently, "Did you think you *were* a sprinter?"

"No! I know I'm not a sprinter. Have you ever seen me run? When they made me run in school, I always pretended to twist my ankle so I wouldn't have to lose so badly. But 'not a sprinter' means there's never any chance that for the rest of my life that will change. No hope. No possibility. Just. Not a sprinter. You know?" They didn't.

Annabel: "Well, you are, like, sixty."

I heard Elias slug her leg under the table.

"It's okay, Elias," I said. "It's not the sprinting. But I'm never going to be a college graduate either."

Elias: "You could. There was a ninety-four-year-old lady that graduated from Emerson last year."

"But that's not going to be me. I have no retention."

Annabel: "It's true. She can't even follow Harry Potter from one movie to the next."

Dayton: "Yeah. She calls them Harry, the girl, and the redhead."

"And I'll never play the piano."

"You could take lessons."

"No, I don't want to. It's a weird time of life. There are more closed doors than open ones. And it messed with me a little. And you guys are out of the house now more than you're in it. And the days of dance parties and us all being together all the time might be past, and I was trying to recapture it. I didn't want to close that door yet."

There was a long pause when I thought they were really getting me. Then Annabel spoke. "You know you were the only one who thought the dance parties were fun, right?"

"I'm going to miss you guys when winter break is over."

They nodded.

"And you're going to miss me."

They didn't nod.

"Say it," I said.

They said it.

"And you're going to miss me when I'm gone."

"Where are you going?"

"Dead. And you know what you'll never say? 'I wish my mom loved me less. I wish she didn't want to spend so much time with me. I wish she didn't put Nutella on my pillow when I came home from college.' You will not spend hours in therapy because your mother spent too much time thinking about what would make you happy."

They nodded again.

"You know what you might say?"

"What?"

"I wish I hadn't said, 'I loved Texas.'"

Then I released the hostages and let them go to their friends or play video games or watch back-to-back TV episodes on their computers. And I washed the dishes.

It's not their fault. It's just nature's unfortunate timing. They are at the time of life when they want to spread their wings. While I am losing my feathers.

Growing Pains

For my fortieth birthday, I went up to the wine country in Sonoma, California, all by myself. With three kids under eight and a show in production, I was never alone. I couldn't wait to eat, sleep, wake up, and go to bed on my own for three glorious days and nights. I stayed at a lovely spa, taking cooking classes during the day and treating myself to various pamperings when I got back to the hotel in the evening. One of these treatments was called a Watsu massage. The brochure said it was their specialty, the ultimate in relaxation, performed by a highly trained Watsu therapist in the hotel's custom-built Watsu pool, heated to the exact temperature of the human body. When I was booking my appointment, the lady at the spa asked whether I preferred a male or female therapist. I didn't want to specify because I was afraid of what the stranger on the other end of the phone would think of me. If I said female, I was afraid she'd think I was uptight because I didn't want a man to touch me, and if I said male, I was afraid she'd think I was a pervert because I wanted a man to touch me. So I said, "Either. Whatever. I'm just doing it for the massage," which definitely made me sound like an uptight pervert.

Andre, my male masseur—thank God because I really wouldn't mind being touched by a man—slipped into the pee-warm pool and laced his arms through mine from behind me. I wore a one-piece Miraclesuit—those bathing suits that promise to make you look fifteen pounds lighter but just make you look fifteen years older. He wore loose cotton yoga shorts—and nothing else.

Andre leaned his head close to my ear and whispered in a soothing/creepy voice, "Lean into me, Kari. Let me support you. I won't let you down." How many times have I heard that?

I tried to do as he said, my back rubbing up against his wet, hairless chest, and he started to rhythmically sway me back and forth in the water. The resistance of the water pulled on my legs, creating a pleasant tension. My wet back and the slight pocket created by the space between Andre's nicely defined yoga pecs made a sucking sound every time they detached at the end of the movement before he swayed me back the other way. I took deep breaths and said a silent prayer for maturity that I wouldn't be overcome by the giggles. I finally started to relax and understand the appeal of this massage: the water, the weightlessness, the strange sensation of having another human being, whom you can't see, supporting you from behind, moving you through the water. It was like a dream, and I started to drift away. Andre could probably feel me letting go and pulled me in tighter to secure me. Now he was more or less spooning me in the water, moving me around the pool, in his arms—the friction between my back and his front increasing, and that's when I felt it: Andre had an erection. It was poking me right in the small of my back through his cotton massage shorts. He didn't stop what he was doing. He didn't change position. He didn't do anything. He just kept Watsu-ing me in the same rhythmic motion as before—but my mind was racing. And, yes, I'm sure it happens all the time. It's certainly a predictable physiological response to rubbing up against someone in a pool for fifty minutes, but to me it felt like a threat, like a holdup, a gun in my back. Because as much as I love nature, I am not one of those "Hey, it's natural" kind of people. I believe if someone farts in yoga, they should stand up, roll up their mat, walk out of the studio, and kill themselves.

All I could think about was the moment when the massage was over, when we would emerge from the pool and Andre and I were going to have to look at each other, both of us knowing what we knew, and that was unacceptable. So I resorted to my failsafe technique for when I'm confronted with awkward, embarrassing, and sometimes even dangerous situations: I pretended I was asleep. My second go-to, which also worked in a pinch, was to fake an intense stomachache. Both of these had been reliable in getting me out of almost all unwelcome, mostly sexually awkward circumstances. I'm reminding you that at this point I was forty. I'd had children. Three. I had a job. A house. I had employees, enough to qualify as a staff, and yet instead of using my voice to express my discomfort, I was pretending to be sound asleep in a swimming pool in Sonoma with a stranger's boner in my back rather than open my mouth and say, "Excuse me, sir; I'm not enjoying my Watsu." And if I was this ill equipped to take care of myself at forty, imagine what a disaster I was at twenty.

When I was twenty, I got what I thought was going to be my big break: a guest star part on the TV show *Growing Pains*, a popular sitcom starring Alan Thicke and Kirk Cameron before he was Christian-crazy. There were five days of rehearsals before we shot the show in front of a live audience. And every day when the producers came down to watch us run through the show, they laughed every time I opened my mouth. Every day when I got my new script, there were more lines for me. I could feel something happening. Something good. And the timing was perfect because I was dead broke.

Alan Thicke was the wise and wry patriarch of the show, Dr. Seaver. If Fred McMurray couldn't be my dad, or Lorne Greene, or Brian Keith, or *Courtship of Eddie's Father*—I'd take him in a heartbeat.

I don't know why all my fantasy dads were parenting without partners . . . why I wanted them all to myself . . . but I'm sure it doesn't mean anything in regards to my relationship with my own father; those things are never very complicated.

On the third day of rehearsal, Alan Thicke approached me at the craft service table. This was it, my big break; I just knew it. He asked me if I had any plans for lunch that day. This was it, my big break; I just knew it. I told him I didn't. I didn't think he needed to know I was going to eat the leftover bagels from the morning because I didn't have any lunch money. He said he'd get me lunch. This was it, my big break; I just knew it. He told me his car was in the shop and he needed to get to his house to check on some construction workers he had there. Did I think I could give him a ride? Was this it? My big break? I didn't know. That was not what I was expecting, but I didn't know what to say except yes. Maybe he was going to talk to me about starring in my own show while I gave him a ride to check on the workers at his house. That was possible.

At lunchtime, we walked out to my forest-green Volkswagen Beetle. I apologized for the mess and tried to clear out the front seat of all the discarded pages from last week's auditions and Del Taco wrappers as best I could. He was tall and classy, and my car was miniature and filthy. His knees were dangerously close to the dashboard, and the seat didn't move. I apologized. Again. And again. And again. He directed me to his house in Encino from the Warner Bros. ranch in Burbank. We made small talk. He mostly asked me questions.

"Where do you live?"

"Venice."

"Where'd you go to college?"

"Didn't."

"Do you have a boyfriend?"

"No."

I drove nervously, very aware of how terrible it would be if I crashed and killed Alan Thicke. Everyone would be so mad at me. I never noticed before how rickety my car was. It was fine for me, but I was carrying valuable cargo now, and it didn't seem like a proper vehicle to transport Dr. Seaver, Mike, Carol, and Ben's lovable dad on the hit show *Growing Pains*.

We finally got to his house. And when we did, I noticed two things. The first was, his house was a mansion. The second was, I didn't see any construction workers. We entered the kitchen, and he offered me something to eat, but I was too nervous. It felt strange to be alone with a big star in his house. I couldn't wait to tell somebody. He didn't mention the workers anymore; he just offered to give me a tour. Which started in his bedroom.

Okay, I want to say right now: there was nothing wrong with me at twenty years old. I didn't have to wear a helmet. I didn't live in my parents' garage. I wasn't on medication. And I wasn't dumb. I wasn't catching on because what was happening was highly inappropriate, and my mind didn't work like that.

Yet. I just thought he liked my acting. And I thought he knew he was old.

So we get to the bedroom, and still, no workers. We were completely alone. He showed me the two-person shower. Nice. Although I've never liked the practice of showering with another person. It takes all the romance out of being naked. And by romance, I mean darkness.

He showed me the balcony that looked out over the massive pool with rock sculptures and waterfalls. He had tiny lights installed in the ceiling of the bedroom—he demonstrated how it looked like the night sky when you turned off all the lights. I could feel him moving closer to me in the pitch black. He was slick and smooth, and I couldn't swallow my spit. I moved away from the sound of his breathing and blurted that I thought we were going to be late getting back to rehearsal and we should go.

On the ride back to the studio, Alan Thicke's mood was unchanged, but I felt completely weird. Then Alan Thicke asked me if I wanted to come with him to the *Growing Pains* wrap party as his date. I felt like a trapped squirrel. I said the first thing that came into my head and told him that I had a boyfriend. Sorry. But thank you for inviting me. Now Alan Thicke's mood instantly changed. His lilting, talk show, "everything I say is kind of a joke" voice wasn't like that anymore, and he snapped back, "You just told me you didn't have a boyfriend."

I stumbled around. "Well, I do actually. I don't know why I said I didn't. But I do. I lie sometimes for no reason. I sometimes tell people I have diabetes, but I don't. My roommate does."

He seemed so mad. But why? Why does Alan Thicke give a shit if I have a boyfriend? He has a TV series and a mansion. I had a Volkswagen full of burrito wrappers and paid for acting class by painting shitty apartments. But then it never occurred to me that this grown-up wanted anything more than a ride to check on his house. Until it did. I thought he was going to offer me a television show. Until he didn't. I thought it was my big break. Until it wasn't.

Disappointed and flustered, I hit a dip in the road too fast and Alan Thicke's knees slammed into the dashboard of my Bug.

He screamed in pain and the word *bitch* came out of his mouth easily. So easily it must have been there all along. He was done with me. We rode the rest of the way in silence, me breathing away tears, his fists balled in rage.

When we walked back on the soundstage, everyone turned to look at us. We were late, and the crew and cast had been waiting. And we were together. Alan Thicke turned back on the talk show smile and cocked his head—giving a look like we'd just walked out of the closet at a Seven Minutes in Heaven party. Several of the crew guys chuckled. I watched the information travel around the set, from one person's knowing eyes to the next. And I felt the heat travel up my neck to my face, like I'd been discovered doing something shameful.

The rest of the week, people still laughed at me, but it didn't feel the same. Kirk Cameron and Tracy Gold, the "kids" on the show, avoided me like fish that had gone bad. When I came in in the morning, they gave each other looks and moved to the far end of the table, making it clear they didn't approve of Alan Thicke's conquest of the week. Problem was, I wasn't.

I made speeches to no one in my car, wrestling back my dignity. Addressing the crew and their dirty minds, setting the record straight. But I knew it didn't matter what I said because I went to his house. Alone. "Why would she do that?" they would ask. Why did I go? Because he was who he was and I was who I was, and before I figured out why I was there, I was staring at stars on the ceiling of his Encino master bedroom. A woman's intelligence is always suspect in these situations. What did she *think* was going to happen? In his mansion. At the spa. In the Watsu pool. What did she want?

Just a job. A massage. A night alone. A big break. Likely story.

The Californian

On the fortieth anniversary of *Saturday Night Live*, Robert De Niro is standing on the stage with his famous smirk telling the story of sometime in his career when he was in LA filming a movie, probably holed up in the Hotel Bel-Air or Chateau Marmont, no doubt making millions—when he turned on *SNL* and saw real work being done in a real city and what a comfort it was to know that this place, New York, and this show, *Saturday Night Live*, existed in the world. It gave him such comfort to know that while he suffered in the soulless shithole that was Los Angeles, they were keeping the dream alive. Or something like that. It might have been a great story if Robert De Niro could tell a story. But he can't. He stumbled over every word. Couldn't find the punch line to save his life, didn't know which words to land on, mumbled through—he was a fucking disaster. It was live television, after all, and if Robert De Niro had to rely on New York theater or live television like *SNL* to make a living, he would starve to death.

I love Robert De Niro, but Robert De Niro clearly needs a script. And some rehearsal. Editors. Takes two, three, four, five, and fifty-seven. Robert De Niro is a movie star, and he should be on his hands and knees thanking Hollywood for taking him in. Thanking the film industry for making him seem articulate and interesting and fluent in English, but instead, he's shitting on the place that made him who he is, which also happens to be my town—which is why I'm mad at Robert De Niro.

Adding insult to injury, I've had a houseguest for the past six days who also happens to be from New York, sleeping in one of my kids' empty rooms.

She leaves wet towels on the wood floors and doors open so my cats escape into the backyard where they could be eaten by Valley coyotes that roam the streets in search of a good meal— usually cat, kitten, or Yorkie. She borrows my car and doesn't refill the gas tank and puts empty half-and-half containers back into my refrigerator as a surprise when I go to prepare my morning coffee.

I don't see her much during the day—she's working in Century City—but when she does come back to the house, I get an earful about the ways in which Los Angeles is not New York while she drinks all my wine on my back porch and asks how long it would take for me to heat the pool.

"A couple of days," I tell her.

She sighs and tells me, "That's the beauty of my health club at the Chelsea Piers. Year-round heated swimming. It's amaaazing."

Grouchy, I ask, "Yeah, but didn't you tell me they have 'poop in the pool' scares several times a year? And it shuts the whole thing down?"

She shrugs as if to say, "Poop is a small price to pay for getting to share a pool with hundreds of strangers in the greatest city on the planet."

I take to hiding in my bedroom in the morning until she leaves for work because I don't trust myself not to heave the empty half-and-half carton at her head if she tells me one more time that she misses public transportation.

My houseguest finally left on Saturday, and I should have felt better, but I didn't. I woke up Sunday, still annoyed. Furious with her, Robert De Niro, and every other disgruntled transplant who complains about LA's lack of seasons, culture, transit, traffic, and lousy bagels. Who eats bagels anymore anyway? Haven't they heard of gluten intolerance? Everyone has it.

I wanted to scream at someone, but in Los Angeles, we don't like confrontation, so we keep it inside and instead have imaginary fights with people from inside our cars, which causes us to have road rage against innocent people who inadvertently cut us off in traffic. So on Sunday, Robert De Niro made me a bad driver. By Monday, the feeling hadn't left me; in fact it was growing. And it happened to be President's Day, so my therapy appointment was postponed until Tuesday, meaning there was nothing to stop my irrational rage at a movie star I didn't know and would probably never meet. Then I started stewing about all the people who complain about LA that I've met in acting classes and in writers' rooms—guys who had come from one-horse towns that had nothing to offer them but subzero winters and tractor-pull summers, and *they* were shitting on LA. "It's not a real city," they'd say, coming from Bumfuck, Wisconsin. I realized my reaction was overblown, and I wondered why. Because it wasn't just a small something stuck in my craw, it was blossoming into full-blown rage-y resentment.

I decided to go to the beach. Maybe that would put me in a better mood. I dragged along my youngest son and my biggest dogs. It took us two and a half hours to drive less than forty miles to Ventura, one of the few beaches that still allowed pets. When we finally got there, we circled the parking lot sixty-three times before we found a spot, then walked to the far edge of the dog-friendly beach away from the dogs who weren't friendly. I found a spot where I wouldn't be able to hear people's inane conversations because I knew that was only going to make me crankier.

I sat watching the seagulls while my kid was fly-fishing in the surf, wading into the low tide waist deep while my dogs chased a tennis ball in the seventy-degree temperature in the middle of February, and it was there I realized the source of my fury: all of these people who hate my California are exactly the ones who have ruined it for those of us who used to love it.

In 1982, I lived in Venice Beach. I was an out-of-work actress who could afford to live at the beach—two houses from the sand. My friends were other actors, and we lived actor lives. We went to scene study class every night and lay on our towels most days. We waited tables and had big dreams. We were every bit as serious as our counterparts in New York. We were just happier. Because we were warm. And tan. And it wasn't so terrible to be poor. Because we were warm. There were pony rides where the massive mall called the Beverly Center is now. A disco called Oskos that was hilarious and easy to get in to. We didn't value places by how hard they tried to keep us out. We had deep conversations about serious subjects—we just happened to be wearing bikinis at the time. I used to drive my 1969 Fiat from my apartment in Venice to my acting class in Hollywood. It would take me about thirty-five minutes. Today that same drive would probably take four days. I'd zip up Fountain Avenue, which was my secret shortcut. There was never a car on it because nobody knew it existed. The San Fernando Valley, where I live now, seemed like the country to us. That was a place you went when you were ready to join AA or have a house with air conditioning or kids.

My friend Brian and I went to every home game the Dodgers played. We called them "three dog nights" because we had to eat three Dodger Dogs each—that was the rule. And we never gained a pound. I also knew where Steve Garvey, the first baseman for the Dodgers, lived. His beach house was right where we set up our towels when we went to the old Malibu Colony during the day. A couple of times, I let my dog, Dudley, a spectacular cocker spaniel and love of my life, off his leash and pretended I couldn't catch him so he would run up the stairs onto Steve Garvey's deck and into his house in pursuit of Steve Garvey's own cocker spaniel—then I would run after him so I could chat up my favorite player, hoping to score free tickets for Brian and me. He never offered any tickets, and after a couple of times, Steve Garvey was on to me and started locking the lower gate that led to the stairs of his beach house.

I sang in an a cappella group, and one year we got one of those maps of the Hollywood stars' homes and went Christmas caroling. Gary Morton enjoyed our performance, but his wife, Lucille Ball, screamed from the top of the stairs, "Tell them to get the fuck away from our house." Glenn Ford answered the door in his pajamas and invited us in. He gave us cookies and, before we left, handed us each a ten-dollar bill and wished us all a merry Christmas. Danny Kaye wasn't well, but he had his caretaker bring him to his balcony in his wheelchair so he could listen to us sing. Which we did, for forty-five minutes. This was when celebrities were great. Before security cameras and electric gates and armed patrols and Kardashians ruined California.

I also blame the Rose Parade. New Year's Day never fails to be gloriously sunny and clear—sparkling blue skies, dotted with just enough white cotton ball clouds to make it festive. The sun glints off our Rose Queen's tiara and her beautiful, young court of princesses wave to the crowd that line Colorado Boulevard in their shorts, T-shirts, and sunglasses on January fucking first, while most of the country watches from their living rooms, dreading the walk outside to let the dog pee in the snow. It never rains on the Rose Parade. It beckons people: Come, you'll be happy here! But they aren't. Because they forget what brought them. Because the grass is *always* greener. And pretty soon they're gathering in groups, with other transplants, at backyard barbecues in March or October or any other day (because it's Southern California and every day is great for a barbecue) to wax nostalgic about what they left behind in their midwestern, East Coast, Canadian, Floridian, New England, northwestern, Upper Peninsulan, Great Lakes, Plains States, Rust Belt, Bible Belt, Dust Bowl–rooted past. "Go home then!" I want to scream. Maybe then I can find a fucking parking place in Venice again. Maybe a shitty ranch house in North Hollywood won't cost a million three. Get. Out.

And by the way, I've been to New York. When my car finally died, I had to review my options. Where could I be an actress without a car? So I moved to New York. Brian knew the manager of a comedy club that had a fairly terrible Mediterranean restaurant upstairs where I got a job as a waitress. I'm a fairly terrible waitress, so it was a good fit. I snagged a $2,000-a-month sublet the size of a closet on the Upper West Side.

I slept all day, too broke for acting class, then went back to the restaurant at night to serve up greasy falafels for minimum wage and no tips. Then winter came. Shivering down the sidewalk, wondering if this was what people missed when they came to LA and complained, "You have no seasons!"

One day my feet slid out from under me on the ice on the sidewalk, my butt landing squarely in a mushy, frozen, and filthy puddle. Not a single person stopped to help me up. They didn't even laugh, which I think was even worse. So I left that city that never sleeps or smiles or says, "I'm sorry," and came back home to thaw out. And it's possible I carried with me a small grudge against the place that didn't welcome me with open arms. People say to me, "You didn't love the energy of the city?" No. I didn't. I didn't love the energy. And then they always make a face that means I'm not cool enough for New York. Which is fine. I'm not cool enough for a lot of things.

I finally got to my therapist appointment. My therapist, Gene, is a native New Yorker who left in 1995 and loves LA so much he thinks the Hollywood Freeway is beautiful. I told him about my rage of the past few days, but as usual, he won't get on board. I think Gene actually used the words *chill out* and started rhapsodizing about the azaleas blooming in February. "Let the LA haters do their worst. We have California," he bubbled. He told me his sister comes out to visit every couple of years and he'll take her to some beachside restaurant. Once they saw dolphins, really close to shore. They watched them for about twenty minutes, jumping and flipping and fooling around, while he and his sister sipped their bottomless mimosas. After the dolphins were gone, his sister turned to him and said, "God, Gene, how do you stand it out here?"

Gravity

I am a loner, a deeply reluctant socializer. I would rather sit in my bed with two dogs and a bowl of popcorn watching *Law and Order: SVU* than be anywhere with anyone that requires me to wear a bra. One or two friends have always been enough for me. In fact, my children as my only friends suited me nicely. Until they left me. The only problem with making your children the center of your social universe is that when they orbit away from you, you find yourself like Sandra Bullock in *Gravity*: spinning in the dark, alone in your underwear, thinking about George Clooney. It also leaves you with no one to reach out to when you need a ride because you're going to be mildly sedated.

On Wednesday, the wind was so powerful it was blowing down palm trees as I made my way to Beverly Hills, creating an obstacle course over Coldwater Canyon. I parked my Prius at a meter on Wilshire and was digging in my purse for quarters when suddenly cash started flying out of my bag, picked up by the wind, then sailing out into the middle of Wilshire

Boulevard. I clutched my purse to my chest and was about to dash into the street after my dollars when a little old man passing by on the sidewalk said in a very calm voice, "Not worth it. Not worth it," then just kept right on walking down the street without even looking up at me. His words stopped me, though. He was right. There were a lot of speeding cars, and it probably wasn't worth it. They were only singles. And only about four had escaped. I stepped back onto the curb, put a credit card in the meter instead, and went into the imaging center for my appointment.

"Routine," Dr. Norman said. "It's important to keep tabs on your uterus during menopause."

"Keeping tabs on my uterus"—this is what it's come to.

Inside there were three people waiting. All old. All yellow. No kidding, I didn't need an MRI to tell me—these people were about to get some bad news. I just hoped they weren't thinking the same about me. I smiled at one lady, but she didn't smile back. So I tried it on the other two people waiting, but all three just stared back at me like they couldn't figure out what I was up to. I pretended to be very interested in something on my phone until they called me into the exam room.

I'll spare you the details of my pelvic ultrasound, but let me say this: anyone who makes their living squirting freezing-cold lube onto a penis-shaped instrument and inserting it into women's vaginas should have a way better sense of humor than my lady did, even if I was the thousandth person to say, "Really? You're not even going to buy me dinner first?" Because that's still funny.

I asked her if she could see anything troubling on the ultrasound. She told me I'd have to wait and get the results from my doctor. I said, "I know, but just tell me this: Based on what you see, what would your advice be for my lunch? Stick to your diet and order the salad, or with the shit I'm seeing in your uterus, you might as well enjoy yourself now and go for the double cheeseburger?" She wouldn't budge. There are some whole days when not a single person is delighted by me.

When I was back at my office, Dr. Norman called right away. I've been seeing him since I was twenty-five years old, and he always has the tone of someone who is about to deliver bad news—loving, serious, and sorry.

Twenty years ago when he told me he saw two heartbeats on my pregnancy ultrasound, I thought he was telling me my baby was going to be born with two hearts, not that I was having twins. It took me a minute to realize the news was exciting, not devastating. Although to be fair, I'm always looking for devastating news, so between his tone and my expectations, we're a disaster together.

This time the news was no news. He tells me they couldn't see anything in the ultrasound. No. Here's what he says exactly: "They got a pretty good view of your giant uterus."

What? Why? Why *giant*, Dr. Norman? No one ever wants to hear the word *giant* used in connection to anything unless it's their brain, vocabulary, or penis. God. It was unkind. I would never say to Dr. Norman, "Oh. Hey. You've got a little something on your giant nose." He said I was going to have to go back for another test. Something called a sonohysterogram. He said the problem was my endometrial lining. They weren't able to see it clearly with the regular ultrasound because due to my age and hormonal changes, it gets quite thick. "Like a shag carpet," he said. And it could be hiding something. Jesus. Giant uterus. Shag carpet? Could you take it easy, Steven?

You know, there was a time when Steven Norman was smitten with me. He would stroke my leg while giving me my pap smear and tell me he would run away with me in a heartbeat. Obviously, that was when my endometrial lining was a gorgeous tightly woven Berber, not a hideously matted shag, hiding old Barbie shoes and green plastic army guys and backs of earrings and God knows what. Was there no end to the indignities of menopause?

"Okay. A sonohysterogram. What's the procedure?" I ask him.

"Well, they inject saline into your uterus—it helps illuminate abnormalities."

"Does it hurt?"

"No."

Right. Of course not. Since I was twenty-five, his only answer to this question has ever been "a little pinch or mild cramping"—that's for everything from cervical dilation to childbirth.

"How much saline goes in?" I inquire.

"Quite a bit. They fill it up like a water balloon."

"And how does it come out?"

"Some comes out right away, when you stand up. That's why they put a pad on the floor."

"Je-sus."

"And the rest comes out over the next forty-eight hours."

"What?"

"Your body releases it."

"When?"

"Whenever."

"Where?"

"Wherever."

Pause.

When my beautiful yellow lab Sophie stopped knowing when poop was dropping from her bottom, I knew it was time to say goodbye. She was much too dignified to live that way. Was no one going to offer me the same kindness?

Dr. Norman tells me he's set it up for Friday at Cedars and I would need a friend to drive me because they would be giving me a mild sedative for the procedure. A friend? Who's going to want to be my friend when I've got salt water dribbling out of my uterus?

That night in bed, I was alone, mulling over what could be hiding in my uterus, when a Facebook message popped onto my computer from someone named Jen Sutherland. I didn't immediately recognize the name. Which happens to me a lot. My dad was a management training executive with the phone company, and we moved every year or two when he got a new assignment, so I was always starting new schools, never staying in touch with the kids I left behind. Because of this, I might have that attachment disorder that orphans get, which is probably why I can't bond to anyone but my dogs and chickens. People remember me though because I used to make up lies about myself to make me seem more interesting, knowing I'd be moving along at the end of the year, leaving only a mysterious memory in my wake. "Remember Kari Lizer? Did you know she could only see in black-and-white?" "Her parents bought her in Haight-Ashbury off a hippie." "They have to move so much because her dad is in the Mafia." "Her middle name is Ferta?"

Jen Sutherland's message said, "Hi. You lived next door to me when I was ten. You told me Santa Claus wasn't real." Oh yeah. I remembered Jen. She had an impossibly thick blonde braid, like a horse, running down the middle of her back.

I was crazy jealous of her because my mom had sent me down to our neighbor Connie's house under the false pretense of borrowing eggs, and Connie, a hairdresser, had ambushed me and given me a pixie haircut.

My mom was tired of me falling asleep with gum in my mouth and waking up with gum in my long hair the next morning—which she then had to try and extract with ice and peanut butter. When Connie was done with me, I looked like the youngest son, Bud, on the TV show *Flipper*. Watching Jen fly around our neighborhood on her bike, her horsey braid flapping behind her, pissed me off. So I told her Santa wasn't real.

Jen had an older sister, Margaret, with a repaired cleft palate, whom I was also jealous of. I wanted something wrong with me that would get me extra attention. I tried in vain to break bones by jumping at odd angles and fast speeds off my skateboard so that I could have a cast for people to sign, but my bones were too strong. I bent paper clips and shaped them into retainers around my teeth so that I could talk with a lisp. My teachers made me take them out of my mouth—saying I was going to swallow them and end up in the hospital—as if I could ever be that lucky. I faked bad eyesight so I could get glasses, but the first day, I sat on them and they broke, and my mom refused to buy me new ones.

Jen had another older sister named Elizabeth, whom I was also jealous of. She was a beauty queen of some sort. I feel like she wore her crown all the time, like around the house and to school, but I can't be remembering that right. She was beautiful, obviously. My dad couldn't shut up about her. Which in hindsight was pretty pervy, since she was sixteen.

All three of those Sutherland girls had something I wanted—amazing hair, harelip, a crown. I didn't care if I was super pretty, super ugly, super deformed, super whatever, I was just not thrilled with being super right down the middle. I normally wouldn't have accepted Jen's Facebook request, but I was feeling vulnerable after my difficult day.

I thought about asking one of the kids to drive me to my procedure, but I knew they wouldn't want to hear about my doctor's visit. The number of appointments for routine screenings seemed to have multiplied into an unmanageable amount in my fifties. As I was leaving for one of those appointments last summer, Dayton said to me, "Another doctor's appointment? Maybe it's time to just let nature take its course." I'm not sure any of them would be the sympathetic ear I needed to share the humiliation I was suffering at the hands of Dr. Norman keeping tabs on my uterus. So I confirmed my friendship with Jen. I quickly looked at my Facebook page to see what kind of impression I would be making on Jen after all these years. Oh shit. My profile picture was the Planned Parenthood logo. Now not only did I kill Santa, Jen would think I had graduated to killing babies. She'd used the word *blessed* twice in her message, so I knew she wasn't going to be on board for that. So even though I knew it was too late, I quickly swapped out the Planned Parenthood logo for a picture of me kissing a donkey in a field of lupine in Vermont. She was going to see that I changed my profile picture five minutes after becoming friends with me, but maybe if I was lucky, she wasn't very Facebook savvy and didn't really realize how the whole thing worked. Maybe I could convince her the Planned Parenthood thing was a pop-up of some sort—a virus that had gotten into my computer without my knowledge. I didn't remember much about Jen, but if she still believed in Santa at age ten, how bright could she be?

I started looking at Jen's adult life as it was represented on Facebook. She had a husband and four kids. All six of them were tan and blonde and fit. Her kids all had Jen's enviable blonde mane of hair.

There were pictures of them on skis and paddleboards, bikes and hiking trails, on boats, in tents. They were playing sports and accepting awards. Her husband was giving a speech to people in suits. Jen was surrounded by a bunch of ladies on a cruise ship in an album called "Besties Cruise the Caribbean." She was with a different group of women in matching T-shirts for a breast cancer awareness walk. And even more women surrounded her at the Cheesecake Factory as she blew out candles on her massive birthday cake. She had so many friends!

I went back to my page and looked again. Me with the donkey. Me with the dogs. Me with a cat. Me with a chicken. People had tagged me on my page too—sending me links to posts showing people who had knit sweaters for their poultry. Or news stories about baby alpacas who got stuck in holes. Deer who made friends with dogs. Dogs who made friends with cows. Cows who made friends with kittens. And nowhere, anywhere, was a picture of me with another human being other than my children. I wondered if this was a problem. I decided to act normal.

I sent Jen a message. "Hey, Jen, nice to hear from you. You look the same. Your family is beautiful. I have three kids, as you can see from my page . . . two are away at college in faraway places. My third is about to go. I'm super proud of them."

The first thing she asks is this: "Are those all your animals?"

I quickly write back, "No! People just like to send me a lot of animal pictures because they know I like animals. I'm kind of an advocate for animals. It's one of my causes." (Trying to sound noble instead of weird.) "I only have three dogs, four cats, six chickens, a rabbit, and two horses."

Jen simply writes back, "Wow." I didn't like her tone.

Then Jen tells me she's moved to Los Angeles for her husband's work and she figured I must live here since I'm in show business. Hey! That's nice. She thinks I'm in show business! I don't think show business even thinks I'm in show business sometimes. She says she thought she'd look me up because she doesn't have a single friend in town. Hey! Me, either! She says maybe we could get together sometime. I ask what she's doing on Friday. Okay. I know.

I'm about to ask a person I haven't seen in more than forty years to drive me to a highly sensitive medical appointment. But here was my problem: Of course I had other friends that I could call, but I couldn't remember the last time I'd actually accepted an invitation to a social engagement from one of them. Also, I'm not great at returning phone calls if I'm not in the mood to talk. There are many days when I don't see or speak to another human. I once went for seven days in Vermont—if I hadn't run out of hummus, who knows how long I would have gone? I'm not just an introvert; I'm actually antisocial. I had turned down so many invitations to parties and plays, dinners and hikes, birthday celebrations, and kids' graduations that I couldn't just pick up the phone now and ask one of those people I'd blown off for months for a favor. Especially knowing that I would probably be back to blowing them off when it was over—and might even ruin the upholstery in their car with my soggy bottom. Damn it, I finally figured out why people needed husbands!

There is one man with a crush on me that cannot seem to be deterred. He'd gladly rush to my aid, even knowing the details of the task. No matter how rude I am to him, he'll still happily take any crumb I throw his way, but I couldn't lead him on, letting him think he had a chance with me by letting him see me sedated and soaked in salt water. Plus, that would probably only make him fall deeper in love with me because seriously, something's wrong with him.

Besides, I justified to myself, Jen is a people person. Look at her Facebook. She walks for breast cancer. She'll probably be happy to help out. So I very gently tell Jen my situation and ask whether she would mind giving me a ride to my appointment and back on Friday. I say we could still catch up on the car ride over to Beverly Hills. And I'll only be mildly sedated on the ride home, so maybe we could stop for a coffee. Unless I need to change my pants. With that I add a little red-faced emoji. I hit send, and I wait for Jen to reply. And I wait. But Jen doesn't reply. I check to make sure my message sent. It did. I check to see if she's still online. She is. And then, a few minutes later, I try to go back to Jen's page, but I can't. Instead, it says, "To add Jen as a friend, send her a request." Jen has unfriended me. Jen has blocked me. I can't believe it. We were only friends for five minutes. Jen was the one who reached out to me! I'm in show business! Shit. I scroll back through our conversation, and my insides curl up because I suddenly realize the inappropriateness of my request, and it makes me want to unfriend myself.

I think it's possible I've gotten so antisocial that I don't know how to interact with people anymore. Not just with Jen, but as I think back over my recent exchanges, I have to consider the possibility that the reason I'm not getting my desired reaction from those I encounter in the world is because I've stopped knowing how to act like a human being and I've become off-putting.

When I smiled at those people in the ultrasound waiting room, maybe I was actually sneering at them. Maybe I drooled. Maybe I spend so much time alone that I don't even know what my own face is doing anymore.

And when I was joking with the ultrasound technician, she wasn't laughing at all. I might not be funny. I walk around my house talking to my animals. And I have voices for my animals so that they can talk back to me. It started as a bit I did with Dayton, but Dayton is never home these days and I'm still doing it. It's not a *bit* if no one is there to see it. It's just cuckoo.

In the movie *Gravity*, when Sandra Bullock was alone in space, she kept it together. She was still cute and witty and charming. That's not me. I'm more *Nell*. Remember that Jodie Foster movie? She grew up alone in the woods? I can't remember what happened to her parents, but Liam Neeson and Natasha Richardson found her and brought her out of the woods. She'd never been around humans before, so she acted like a wild animal. Super inappropriate. Like me. I'm Nell. Not Sandra Bullock. Nell.

I leave Dr. Norman a message on his answering service, and he calls me back right away. I tell him I can't have the sonohysterogram on Friday. When he asks why, it's hard for me to get the words out because I'm afraid I'm going to sob—hard and loud. I can't trust myself to behave in a socially acceptable way anymore—God only knows what kind of animal sounds could escape. So I whisper, "I don't have a friend to drive me home." There's a long pause, then Dr. Norman tells me he's going to be at Cedars-Sinai on Friday and he'll be happy to drive me home after my procedure. For some reason, I'm not mortified by this. I'm happy. I love Dr. Norman. I'm comfortable with him. We've been through everything together—me trying not to get pregnant, me trying to get pregnant, pregnancy, childbirth, trying not to get pregnant again, now this motherfuckery called menopause—and he's always been about eight years ahead of me on the path, warning me about the happiness and the heartbreak. I was in the stirrups, mid–gynecologic exam, when he broke down over his only child leaving for college. I had to reach down between my legs and pat the top of his head to comfort him. Truth is, my gynecologist is my longest and possibly healthiest relationship. He's my best friend. I thank him and tell him I'd run away with him in a heartbeat. He doesn't say anything. Awkward.

After we hang up, I resolve to get out of the house more. Connect to people more. Show up for my friends. Maybe I'll start throwing dinner parties. Or host play readings at my house. I could build a little stage in the backyard and put twinkle lights in the trees. I won't just be social, I'll be artsy. And effortlessly chic. I think I'll wear kaftans and big wooden earrings from Cost Plus. I decided to reach out to a few friends right away and get the ball rolling.

As I'm deciding who to call first, I look up at the TV. The *Law and Order: SVU* episode with Rob Lowe and Margot Kidder is on. Oh my God, that is such a good one. The first one with Dr. Huang. I love Dr. Huang. I tell the dogs I wish he was my psychiatrist. I speak for Canelo Alvarez, my boxer, who says, "You could use him," in his Spanish accent. I decide it's too late to call anyone right now, summon the dogs on the bed, and turn up the volume.

I Am the Best Person Ever

Los Angeles is a city filled with judgmental people. Everywhere I go, I can feel myself being assessed, from my car to my clothes to my skin. I'm a single mom—my car is dirty, I sometimes buy my clothes at Whole Foods, and I've been known to cut my own hair when the chardonnay tells me it's a good idea. Because of that, I'm forever being misjudged. And I hate being misjudged more than just about anything. Whether it's a stranger interpreting my bad driving as bad manners or a long-lost friend from high school telling people I'm stuck-up because I can't get her tickets to *Ellen*—no one can get tickets to *Ellen*! I get in fake arguments all day long, making my case to my rearview mirror, defending my honor against injustice. Because it's important to me that people know: I'm a really good person. When I realized a long time ago that I'd never be the best looking or the smartest or the richest or the classiest or the most successful or the smartest, I decided to be the most decent. I decided to be the best person ever, which honestly, isn't that hard to do in Los Angeles.

I'm a naturally guilty person. When I was in the fourth grade, I kept a notebook by my bed, and when the trespasses of the day kept me awake at night, I'd make a list of the amends I'd make the next day to soothe myself: Tell Debbie Nunes I lied, I don't have a palomino stallion that I keep at my grandma's house in Spokane that won't let anyone touch him but me because he's a wild mustang. Don't let Jimmy Ballard reach under your shirt again, even if he makes you give back his ID bracelet. Stop smoking cigarettes with Cheryl Liston.

Stop taking sips of Cheryl Liston's beer. Stop listening to Cheryl Liston's stories about the sex stuff she does when the dad drives her home from her babysitting job. Stop hanging out with Cheryl Liston.

I still have a notebook by my bed, but since I decided to be the best person ever, I don't need to use it as much as I used to, though I still have the occasional off day. I didn't grow up with people servicing me, so I'm already uncomfortable sitting in the giant white leather mani-pedi chair at my semi-regular nail salon, Soothe You Spa. As much as I love walking into Soothe You Spa with my dried-out, nail-bitten fingers and cracked-heel, dirt-in-the-crevices feet and walking out looking like a person who lives in an industrialized country, the act of tolerating a mostly non-English-speaking immigrant washing and scrubbing my feet, picking out the corners of crud while I'm supposed to flip through *People* magazine, is uncomfortable. It also seems vaguely racist. It's why I overtip, overthank, and overexplain my reasons for being there. "Sorry," I say to Kim-Li, "my hands are terrible. I wash a lot of dishes, and I never remember to wear gloves." For some reason, it seems better to me if she knows I wash dishes. See? I have to do gross things too. Not remove toe lint from strangers' feet, but I definitely have stuff. I also explain that my feet are nasty because I go barefoot when I let my chickens out in the morning. And I camp. And I'm a single mom. "I'm not here to pamper myself. I'm such a mess, this service is practically a medical necessity."

Kim-Li is using the scraper on my big toe callus, and she doesn't care. She starts up a lively conversation with her coworker at the next chair, who is lotioning up the calves of a young, tan, fake-boobed girl. I notice that the girl's skin glistens, obviously waxed from stem to stern. Like a hairless Chihuahua. I forgot to shave my legs.

"I'm a single mom!" I protest in my head. "I can't do everything!" The shiny, clean girl sits in her chair, thoroughly unbothered as she flips through *US* magazine and compulsively checks her iPhone for activity, even though she's sitting right under a sign that asks you not to use your cell phone in the salon. I try to give Kim-Li a look that will communicate to her that I don't approve of the Chihuahua's flagrant disregard of the rules, hoping to put us on the same side against the girl, but she's busy chatting with her friend. And I'm suddenly positive that my nail lady is asking the next-door nail lady why she always gets stuck with the gross ones, and it hurts my feelings. I could look shiny and clean too, if I had nothing to do all day but tend to myself and all I cared about was my looks. But I care about important things, like global warming. That dumb, beautiful, hairless girl probably hasn't thought about the planet all day. I'll bet she drives a Range Rover, while I sit in my plug-in Prius even though the seats are so uncomfortable they leave me with a pinched nerve in my sacrum. But I do it for the earth. I also recycle. And compost. I pulled up all my grass for the drought and put rocks in my yard and scraggly "indigenous" plants that look like weeds that grow next to a freeway. And I'm a single mom! God, that awful girl is pretty. She must not have any problems.

The girl catches me staring at her, so I pretend to be interested in something just over her shoulder. I look out the large shop window at busy Ventura Boulevard and see a homeless man, pushing a broken-down bicycle, making his way up the sidewalk toward the salon. A giant black trash bag is balanced on the basket of his bike. It's stuffed full of, I assume, all the man's worldly possessions.

The man is so filthy, I honestly can't tell whether his skin started out white or black or something in between. His hair is full of mats that kind of look like dreadlocks but are not a style choice. His ankles are exposed between his taped-up Converse low tops and the ragged bottoms of his . . . jeans? Khakis? They're so covered in grime it isn't possible to know what color his pants started as either. His ankles are hideously swollen, angry purple where the skin is stretched to its limits from poor circulation. Like they're about to pop. It makes his feet look tiny and out of proportion beneath them. Kim-Li looks away from my feet and up at him, probably thinking he's my boyfriend coming to pick me up—since it looks like he camps too.

He shuffles more than walks, and every slide looks painful. He stops in front of the door to the salon and seems to be studying the business hours posted there. After several minutes, he opens the door and, leaving his bike and belongings alone on the sidewalk, enters the salon. There are only four customers inside with about six employees, and everyone stops talking and looks at the man. The owner, Rick, a young, thin, soft-spoken, and sweet Vietnamese man, moves quickly from the back of the room to the front. The homeless man speaks in an inappropriately loud, scratchy voice to no one in particular. "Can I have some money?"

Rick is now about five feet away from him, and that's where he stops, not looking confident that he can handle this situation up close. Rick tells him, in a slightly shaky voice, "You can't do that here, man."

But the homeless guy walks farther into the salon, not even looking at Rick, and asks the hairless Chihuahua, "Can you give me some money?"

The girl drops her eyes to her magazine, ignoring the request. The man turns to the rest of us and asks us as a group, "I need money. Can you give me some money?"

The other two customers are private school mom types in their forties—the kind who don't look like they exercise but wear nothing but yoga pants and who had been talking about what they were going to eat for lunch for thirty solid minutes, pretending they were going to be "good" on their diets, but every time they mentioned Mexican food, gasped and giggled, "That would be so bad!" They were clearly each other's enablers, and there was not a chance these two weren't going to be eating nachos with the works as soon as their nails were dry enough to get them to Poquito Mas. They both shake their heads and also avert their eyes from the homeless man. The women working on our feet watch the man but show no opinion about him—not fear or anger. And he doesn't address them; I guess he knows they already have it hard enough, scrubbing white women's feet for a living.

The man turns to me and says again, "I need money." And his eyes stay on mine. I don't look away.

I say, "I'm sorry. I don't have any cash." It's not true, but I'd already played out my best move in my head. If I was going to give him cash, that would entail me taking my feet out of the suds in the foot tub, sliding out of the giant chair, fetching my purse from the floor next to the chair, and locating an appropriate amount of cash without letting him see exactly how much I had access to. It seemed labor intensive and fraught with opportunities for an escalation of the already uncomfortable situation.

He doesn't move on; he just keeps staring at me, I guess, because I'm his last hope. So I say again, "I don't have any cash." Then I try to say with my eyes, "But I'm a very good person who cares about the homeless." And I give him a little smile.

He takes a step closer and, with so much anger the whole salon registers an extra heartbeat, says, "You stupid rich bitch, don't laugh at me." Then he shuffles out of the salon, retrieves his bicycle, and continues down the street.

Everyone in the salon lets out a breath. The private school moms laugh. Rick apologizes. The Chihuahua says with a sneer,

"I hate that they can just walk in anywhere they want to." The fake yoga ladies nod their heads in agreement.

"They?" I say. "By *they*, do you mean human beings?" Okay. I don't say that. But I think it. Hard. Hairless Chihuahua goes back to her magazine article about Nicole Kidman's private heartbreak. The moms go back to chatting about what they're going to eat, deciding that after that little scare, they definitely deserve a cheat day. Kim-Li goes back to declawing my feet, but I'm shaky. I am not a rich bitch. I'm a good person. I'm a single mom! I'm probably the nicest person in this place. How could he not see that? I had been misjudged in the most horrible way possible.

Why do I care what that unstable man thought of me? Why do I care if the lady at my feet thinks I'm gross or spoiled or a racist? I know what I am. Who are they to judge me? Why does it bother me? I sit with that a minute, then realize, oh, I know. Because that's what *I* do. I judge everyone. All the time. I'm constantly assessing people and determining who and what they are based on the smallest amount of information. And I really don't like it when someone does it to me. I wanted to tell the homeless man about my volunteer work and compost bin. Of course the homeless man would probably really think I'm an asshole then.

I decided the poor girl next to me must be shallow and fake and without a brain in her head because she likes to wax all her hair off. So what?

Maybe she has a problem with excessive hair growth. I don't know. And the private school moms. I have no idea if their kids go to private school. They might not even have kids. For all I know, they're infertile, so they talk about food all the time to fill the hole. By the way? *My* kids go to private school, so fuck me. And so what if they wear yoga clothes—they probably go to yoga. Or they probably *mean* to go to yoga. I wear running shoes, and I don't run anywhere. And Rick—I don't even know if he's Vietnamese. I assigned him a nationality. And why do I think he's nice just because he's Asian? Maybe he's an asshole. Maybe he beats his wife. And maybe Kim-Li likes her job. Maybe she's proud of her ability to transform ugly feet and hands into ugly but well-groomed feet and hands. Why am I feeling sorry for her? Because *I* think her job sucks. Because *I'm* the misjudger. Me. Miss Judgy. I think everyone from the South is a racist and every guy in a fraternity is a rapist. I think all Republicans are homophobes and anyone who doesn't like dogs is untrustworthy. I think pretty girls can't be funny. And handsome guys can't be faithful. That's terrible. What's wrong with me? Could it be that I'm *not* the best person ever?

Kim-Li is done with my toes. She thanks me and scoots her rolling stool to the next chair. Maybe in a hurry to get away from me. But maybe not. I don't know her. I don't even know where I got the idea that her name was Kim-Li. Did she ever actually tell me that?

I have to get out of there. I delicately walk over to Rick, try-ing not to dislodge the toilet paper that's keeping my toes sepa-rated, pay my check, with a regular-sized tip—what's-her-name doesn't need my 40 percent pity tip—then walk out of Soothe Me Spa and onto Ventura Boulevard, hating myself.

I look down the sidewalk in the direction that the homeless guy went to see whether he is still in sight. I don't see him. I unlock my Prius, which I drive because I think people will have the right impression of me, and pull away from the salon. I see him about two blocks down. The homeless man has leaned his bike and belongings against a storefront for lease and laid him-self down on the sidewalk to sleep. His back is turned to me, and I can see that his shirt has split all the way up, exposing his skin. It's cold outside, one of those days where everyone in Los Angeles talks about how cold it is because we always forget that happens here. The guy must be freezing. I pull into the next metered space that I see and get out of my car. I open the hatch-back and pull out the down coat I keep back there for emergen-cies. An old crew jacket from *Weird Science*. I could probably get decent money for that on eBay (not something the best person ever would think). I also grab the pair of soccer socks one of the kids has left behind and a bottle of Gatorade. I take a twenty from my purse.

I walk to the man and stand a few feet away. I say, "Excuse me, sir." He doesn't move. I step a bit closer and say more loudly,

"Hello?" Nothing. I put the twenty into the pocket of the coat and step even closer. I bend down, laying the coat over the man's exposed back. I set the Gatorade bottle next to him, and the socks near his feet, hoping he isn't going to spring awake and stab me repeatedly.

I'm a good person. Well, I'm a flawed person, but I'm always engaged in a struggle in my head and heart to be a *better* person, and that's got to count for something. I stand up and look down the street. About a block away, there are four guys in suits coming out of the Starbucks, heading toward me.

I have a thought. Am I still the best person ever if nobody sees me being the best person ever? I mean, even the homeless guy slept through my generosity.

I know I won't look back at this moment proudly, but I crouch back down next to the homeless guy and pull the coat off his back. As soon as the guys are close enough to notice me, I return the coat to the homeless man's exposed back, patting him gently. I adjust the Gatorade bottle and socks. By now, the guys are right there, and they've stopped to watch. I look up, as if I'm surprised by their presence, and say, "He looked cold."

One of the guys says, "That's really cool, man. You're a nice lady." I shrug modestly and walk back to my car.

It's not a perfect act of kindness, but I think I get points for being aware of how imperfect it is. I mean, most people don't even question their behavior because most people are jerks, I say to my rearview mirror as I pull away. "You're fine. You're fine," I say, soothing myself. But I know what will be going in the notebook next to my bed in the middle of the night: "Give anonymously."

The Art of Self-Defense

My story starts in Amsterdam. My daughter and I met up there for a three-day holiday while she was going to school in Scotland. On the second morning of our trip, we decided to take a cruise through the canals. Our guide was Eddie, a retired sea captain in the Dutch Royal Navy, but now, in his midseventies, Captain Eddie spent his time piloting a restored 150-year-old barge around the canals of Amsterdam, sharing the city's rich history with his eight or so passengers. Annabel and I were on the first tour of the morning. Captain Eddie helped us into the boat by offering his hand, warning us not to hit our heads on the low ceiling. He was tan and fit, with sparkling blue eyes and that indeterminate Dutch accent. We chatted with Captain Eddie while waiting to be joined by the other passengers: two older couples—one from America, one from Ireland—and a mother, father, and fourteen-year-old daughter from Singapore. After our safety briefing, we pulled away from the dock, and the tour commenced.

Our captain began describing his city with colorful stories of Nazis and immigrants and plague, and as he was talking, I became increasingly aware that the only person Captain Eddie seemed to be speaking to was me. It was like I was the only one on the boat. I would look away for a minute, only to turn back and have him staring directly into my eyes.

The Irish lady held her hand up for a full five minutes with a question, but Captain Eddie never called on her—he was too busy with my personal tour, only looking away from my face to make sure the barge was still on course, then turning back to me, just me, with a nod and a cap-toothed smile. When he'd reveal something slightly scandalous about the city, he'd wink, like we had an inside joke. He asked me if I wanted to drive the boat or climb onto the bow to take better pictures. He didn't make that offer to anyone else, even though the Singapore teenager was stuck taking pictures from inside, where there was nothing to photograph but the glare from the windows. Annabel noticed my special treatment, too, and began to call him "Captain New Daddy." Captain New Daddy mentioned at least twelve times that Amsterdam was a liberal city. And when he said it, it was always directed at me with special emphasis on the word *liberal* that made it seem like he was saying, "I'll get you down on all fours and fuck you right here." When we went past the barge where the city collected stray cats, he referred to it as the *pussy boat* and licked his lips at me in a way that made my neck sweat. The young girl from Singapore looked at me like I must be one of those Amsterdam whores she'd heard so much about. A few minutes later, I looked up and she was taking my picture. This went on for two hours and ten minutes until finally I'd perspired through my bra and the tour was over. Captain New Daddy handed me his personal card, saying he'd love to see me again. I thanked him and hurried off the boat, hitting my head on the low ceiling on my way out, wondering what would happen if I did call him. It had been so long since I'd engaged in anything that casual, I actually considered it. Maybe when Annabel gets on the plane back to Scotland, I should give Captain New Daddy a call and just see what he's got in mind for me. Of course I wouldn't.

One of the problems with being morbidly addicted to crime dramas was that all roads in the imagination lead to violent death. It's why I'll never online date or carpool or eat the samples at Costco.

When I got back home, I told Gene the shrink about the unusual number of romantic opportunities I had in Europe. When I petted the Frenchman's dog and he asked if I would do the same to him. The waiter who gave me free wine and offered Spanish lessons in his apartment. And finally, Captain New Daddy. Europe Me was so much more popular than American Me. But of course I didn't act on any of my offers, I assured him.

My therapist asked, "What if you did? Not the one-night stands, but something more promising. Can you imagine love at this point in your life?"

"No. I don't even know what love is."

"Oh, come on. You have lots of love in your life."

"Sure," I said, "lots of unrequited love."

"That's not true," he said, practically scolding me, which is something he does when I get determined to be hopeless and heartless. "What about your children?"

"That's worse than unrequited. That's mercy-fuck love."

Gene clutched his pearls. He likes to pretend he's more delicate than he is when I pretend to be more jaded than I am.

I continued anyway. "I want to eat them alive, know their every thought, be part of every moment of their lives, and they stay just connected enough to me to keep their bank accounts open."

He kept his eyes steady on me, waiting for me to be less dramatic or at least tell the truth.

"Okay," I admitted, "they love me. But they aren't desperately *in* love with me like I am with them. Of course. Thank God. That wouldn't be normal. Nobody wants that. Except me."

"Okay. So try to imagine grown-up love now. Romantic love. What would that look like? Try to remember that warm, fuzzy feeling and how that might be for you."

Why? Why does everyone think that if you aren't in a relationship you're walking around with a hole in your heart? I closed my eyes, trying hard to think how it might go. I would meet this man, and we would hit it off. Things would progress. We would become a *we*. We'd start spending all of our time together. Then what? Would we move in together? Whose house would we live in? Well, I'm not leaving my house. Okay. So he moves into my house. What if he didn't like my dogs? Or my cats? Or my chickens? Would we take vacations? What if he hated traveling? What if I love him more than he loves me, or worse, he loves me more than I love him? No. I can't do this! I broke up with my imaginary new boyfriend and declared it impossible. My therapist is staring at me and quiet. What?

"Do you think it's possible that you've become too self-protective to allow anybody in and that's why you're alone?"

"No. That's stupid. I just told you, I got propositioned all over Europe."

He continued to watch me. And annoy me.

Because *anyone* who is involved in a partnership believes that *everyone* wants to be involved in a partnership. Even if their own partnership is a misery, which I'm assuming Gene's is because at this point, he's bugging the shit out of me and I'm not even his wife.

They really truly believe that when someone says, "I like being alone," it only means, "I haven't found the right person yet," or "I'm afraid of getting hurt," when sometimes it just means, "I like being alone." And I find my best place to be alone is Vermont. So I told Gene we were taking a break while I went to Vermont to be alone. I promised him I'd think about why I was alone, while I was alone, enjoying being alone.

When I get to Vermont this time, Tom, the seventy-year-old native Vermonter who takes care of my place, tells me he has a surprise for me. A little early birthday present. He bought me a gun. Shit. I hate guns. I sign petitions against guns. I write Facebook posts complaining about guns and the people who own them. Tom tells me he'd feel better about me living all alone up in the woods if I had a gun. He did it because he loves me. And I couldn't say anything because I love Tom, and also he just finished a course of chemo for colon cancer, and I was so happy to see him up and about, if he told me he bought me a mink stole, I'd probably just suck it up and wear it into town. So I said, "Thank you." And he said he was going to teach me how to use it.

We took my four-wheel-drive Gator into the woods to find a suitable place for my shooting lesson. Tom brought along a paper target attached to a wooden stick. He pulled my brand-new .38 Smith & Wesson Special out of its box. It was shiny and pretty in a way, I guess. He took out a box of bullets and explained he got me hollow points because "they make a hole in your target like an extra-large pizza."

"Why do I want that?" I asked.

He told me I'd be happy to have them if a bear was coming at me.

"I'm not going to shoot a bear, Tom! I love bears. If I shoot anything, I'm shooting a person." He ignored me and dumped my giant, deadly bullets out of the box. His hands were shaky, and the bullets kept getting away from him, dropping on the ground and rolling away.

"What's happening there?" I asked him.

"The chemo makes my darn fingers numb. Can't get a grip on the bullets," he told me.

"Maybe this isn't the best day for a shooting lesson."

He laughed. "Don't worry. Nothing's going to happen."

Sure. When did you ever hear of something going wrong with a gun? He finally got the bullets loaded, showed me how to cock the hammer and where to put my fingers, then told me to give it a try. Shaky myself now, I stood about twenty feet from the target and raised the gun.

Tom stopped me. "You want to aim down, if you can. If you shoot up in the air like that, them bullets will travel two miles. You could kill something."

Terrified, I shot that thing five times and had to stop. It was so loud my ears were ringing, and I could tell my shoulders were going to be sore in the morning from the kickback. But I hit that target three times. "Good enough," I told Tom. He agreed. That bear would be deader than dead. I replaced the word *bear* with *rapist* in my head and was surprised when I felt a little bit of that warm, fuzzy feeling Gene was talking about in California.

That night, when I went to bed, I brought the gun and bullets up to my room to hide them in safe and separate places. I pulled the drawer of a built-in dresser all the way out and placed the gun on the floor, then replaced the drawer over the top of it.

I took the box of bullets to the other side of the room where there was an armoire and shoved them underneath so they couldn't be seen from anywhere in the room. Then I went to bed. I was almost asleep when I was brought back to wide awake by a loud noise somewhere downstairs. I sat up in bed, immediately and completely alert, and listened, the hair standing up on my arms like antennae. Barely breathing, I waited. It happened again. My reasonable brain tried to tell me, "What are the odds that someone would be breaking into your house the very first night you own a gun? Isn't paranoia a more likely conclusion?" Then something banged again, and I crawled out of bed toward my gun.

As quietly as I could, I removed the drawer that concealed my weapon. I felt around in the dark until my hand landed on it. I gripped it the right way, muzzle pointing away from me, then scooched across the floor on my butt to where my ammo was stored. Another loud sound from downstairs made me jump and turn quickly toward the bedroom door, pointing my empty gun into the darkness. After a moment, I relaxed and retrieved my bullets from the armoire. I went over to the side of my bed farthest from the door. I dumped the bullets onto my bed, and though I'd only had one lesson and could barely see my own hand in front of my face in the moonless Vermont night, I was able to feel my way and release the chamber, slide the bullets into place, and secure the barrel back into position. My gun was loaded. Kneeling on the wood floor, the bed between me and the door, I pointed the gun at the door, steadying my arms on the mattress, leaning my body against the side of the bed, mostly hidden from view, my gun trained on whoever might come through that doorway. They would be walking into an ambush. Then I waited.

Sometimes stress makes me sleepy. When I have a script due and I can't figure out the story, I get stress sleeping sickness. As the deadline approaches, I find myself unable to keep my eyes open at my desk. It's like a recurring nightmare I used to have where I'm the star of a play, but I keep falling asleep when it's time for my lines.

When I woke up the next morning, I was still in my defensive position, sitting on the floor, behind my bed, in my April Cornell nightdress. My .38 Smith & Wesson Special, loaded with hollow point bullets, was on the bed within easy reach, the sounds of distant thunder fading and the barn doors still banging on the front of the house from the wind. Oh. It was the barn doors. No unlucky stranger had entered in the night.

I tried to stand on my useless legs, which had fallen asleep from being bent underneath me on the wood floor all night long. I couldn't turn my head—my neck muscles had seized up from the tension and kickback of the target practice the day before. I moved slowly to the bathroom, half crawling like a crippled sand crab. I looked back at my gun, resting on my giant empty bed, and I had to consider Gene's words: "Do you think it's possible you've become too self-protective to allow anybody in?" I decided to give up my gun and go back to therapy.

Want

———

I stared at the email from the hostess of the dinner party I promised to attend. She was asking that I bring an appetizer, something without cheese or gluten, preferably. She had copied the other invitees, so I could see who else I'd be spending the evening with, each name producing an involuntary *uch* from the back of my throat: the former network executive who now produces reality TV and asks too many questions about "what I've got in the hopper"; the actor couple I'd met a thousand times who nonetheless always say, "Nice to meet you," as they're looking past me for someone famous or at least better looking; the real estate shark with the giant teeth who corners me about the recent sales in my neighborhood and can't believe I still live in the Valley when I could afford "to actually live someplace nice"; plus a few new people who have been added to the roster with whom I'll have to start from scratch, comparing how many people, exercise routines, childhood tragedies we have in common—exhausting—like starting with a new therapist. And then, the hostess herself, a woman I've known for more than thirty years, who plans these dinner parties on a bimonthly basis with a rotating guest list of mismatched semifriends sitting around discussing which food-elimination diet they're on and how it's changed their lives. I used to be a regular attendee, but I'd stopped showing up. In fact, I'd stopped showing up a lot of places—birthday parties, book clubs, one-man shows—and people were starting to notice.

I always RSVP in the affirmative because everything sounds like fun when it's more than a month in the future; plus I never really expect to live that long. But when the day actually arrives, I find myself hoping for a slight case of shingles.

I also knew that if I blew this dinner off, I'd probably find myself off the guest list permanently, which I wouldn't have minded, except that Gene the shrink said studies have shown that retreating from social interactions as one ages may lead to dementia or early death. I just wish I knew which one.

I stood in my closet, incapable of getting myself dressed, a heap of discarded linen tunics from the Gap lying at my feet. Boyfriend jeans hung on my hips, not looking androgynous and hippie carefree like I'd hoped when I bought them two sizes too big—they just made my legs look too skinny, like a woman who should get her bone density checked. I found myself whining into my mirror, "I don't want to go!" I have been doing way too many things I don't want to do lately, and why do I have to? It was a thought that had been with me ever since my friend came over with her baby a few days before.

As they came in the door, my friend, Amy, looking wild-eyed and overwhelmed, gestured toward her darling daughter, dressed all in purple with two tiny high ponytails bobbing on top of her head like a Pixar cartoon character, and warned me, ominously, "She's two next week. It's a whole new thing." As we moved into the living room, she turned to the almost-two-year-old Jemma and asked, "Do you want to give Kari a hug?"

"No," Jemma said, not ambiguously.

And so it began.

Amy continued in a voice that quivered with desperation: "Do you want to try a little fruit?"

"No!"

"Do you want to sit on Mommy's lap?"

"*No.*"

Girl knew what she wanted. And it wasn't anything her mother was offering. Amy kept apologizing, looking shell-shocked by this new phase of development her formerly mute and docile infant had entered into, but I was intrigued. Jemma proceeded to touch every piece of watermelon in the serving dish and not eat a single one, then place her sticky hands on the upholstered muslin chair, then take a swipe at the cat before sticking her hand deep into her diaper where she felt around for something interesting before dancing that same hand over the cheese plate before spontaneously placing a kiss on her mother's knee. Just because she wanted to. And for the next two hours, Jemma didn't do a single thing she didn't want to do: she didn't pee in the toilet, she didn't smile or say her newly learned ABCs, she didn't high-five, sit on the couch, be careful, play gentle, say please, leave the piano alone, put down the candle, put down the glass, put down Mommy's purse, stop touching Mommy's phone, stop touching Kari's hair, show everyone how you can dance, show everyone how you can sing, show everyone your teeth. Where's your nose? Where're your toes? Where's your tummy? Jemma wasn't telling.

And I wasn't horrified. All I thought was that at fifty-seven years old, I wouldn't mind returning to my terrible twos. Jemma was my role model.

Doing exactly as I want and, more importantly, not doing anything I don't want to do. What could be wrong with that?

No, I don't want to tell you what I'm working on, using on my skin, eating for breakfast.

No, I don't want to listen to your advice about my allergies, career, personality, finances, or astrological sign.

I don't want mirrors in my house.

I don't ever want to wear high heels again.

Or false eyelashes.

I don't want to wear false anything.

Or lip liner.

Or body glitter.

Or anything that's tight around my stomach.

I don't want to "just try" cashew butter. Or cashew cheese.

I don't want to go out to eat with people who study the check in order to determine which one of us owes a dollar thirty more than the other. "Who had the side of fruit?"

I don't want to hear about your "amazing guy" and CBD colonics.

I don't want to be in writers' rooms with fifty-year-old white men who talk about where they went to college. Or camp.

If my mother asks if I've found a job yet or have any "interviews" this week because after thirty years she still doesn't understand the nature of being a writer or the concept of being self-employed, I don't want to explain it to her again—I want to drop my phone in the toilet.

I don't want to go to parties with strangers or people who ask me things that are none of their business, like, "Hey, how much money did you end up making on that last show?" Which is the adult equivalent of "Show me your tummy." And I don't want to. Just like I don't want to answer anyone who asks me, "Did you ever think about trying to write movies instead of just TV?" "What are Will and Grace really like?" "Was Andy Griffith a racist?"

If anyone—and I mean *anyone*—is more than five minutes late for an appointment, lunch, or date with me, I don't want to wait for them or reschedule.

I don't want to hug everyone I meet. I don't want to ever fist-bump anyone.

I don't want to get Brazilian bikini waxes or wear thong underwear.

I don't want to wear anything that requires undergarments to flatten my stomach or unflatten my ass. I don't want to fast unless I'm getting a colonoscopy. I don't want to.

I don't want to.

I don't want to make small talk or act interested in boring people.

I don't want my boobs lifted or vagina reconstructed.

I don't want to bite my tongue when someone says something racist or classist or sexist.

I don't want to be polite when my friends are married to assholes.

I don't ever want to buy something because someone tells me it will regrow my collagen or my hair or my eyelashes.

I don't want to spend more than forty dollars on face cream.

Which has left me to think about what I *do* want.

I want to start wearing overalls again.

I want to figure out how to keep my room the perfect temperature.

I want hummingbirds outside my window.

I want three dogs at all times.

I want friends who are younger than me and older than me.

I want to go for days without thinking about what I look like.

I want to sleep.

I want to never feel jealous again.

I want to sit at tables—dinner tables and writing tables and farm tables—with people who make me laugh.

I want people to tell me the truth.

I only want to know men who truly love women.

I only want to know women who love other women.

I only want to know women and men who love dogs.

I want to have a goat.

Me on All Fours

Animal people are nuts. You know it's true if you've ever tried to adopt a cat from a rescue organization. Despite the fact that they are quite literally crawling with dozens of unwanted scrawny felines, when you try to take one home, they say, "Not so fast. You first need to fill out this fourteen-page application and supply three references and a credit check, and then we'll make a home visit to determine if your residence is cat worthy." Not a single question was asked when I decided to become a parent—and there really should have been some questions. I pursued my acting career instead of going to college and was cast as a cheerleader more than any other character, even though in real high school I was rejected as even the mascot. I believed the only way to get another job was to spend all the money from my last job, and I shifted from acting to writing because a psychic named Teresa Giappatros told me to after feeling the vibrations in my keychain. Yet less than thirty-six hours after giving birth via C-section to my twins, the nurse simply rattled off instructions to me about nipple care and latching on, fevers, and infected umbilical cords . . . me still in my postbirthing daze, not able to focus on anything but how to talk them into sending me home with that delightful morphine drip. My partner in parenthood, Jack, undoubtedly still traumatized from seeing my innards taken out of my abdomen and set aside on the operating table, probably wasn't retaining much of the information either.

Nevertheless, they just placed those two humans, one in the crook of each arm, wheeled us to the underground parking lot, casually looked to make sure the car seats were facing the right direction, and sent us on our way. We could have driven off and sold them, for all they knew. We could have used the money.

But somehow the children lived, and we even added another, and again, no one checked to see whether this was a good idea. They just let us do it. As my children grew and became more self-sufficient—well, not self-sufficient, just less interested in spending time with me—the marriage went by the wayside, and the demands of my career ebbed and flowed, I found myself looking for meaningful ways to spend my time. If you live in LA and work in show business, it's important sometimes to do things that remind you of what's real. I needed places other than motherhood and Hollywood to give me purpose and per-spective. I found that place in Friends on Four Paws.

Friends on Four Paws is a therapy dog organization that sends volunteers and their pets to hospitals, schools, old folks homes, special events—any place where the presence of a sweet dog could alleviate stress, facilitate healing, or bring a smile. It's a wonderful organization that visits more than eighty facilities in and around Los Angeles. It's filled with committed animal people who generously donate their time to a very worthy cause. What I quickly discovered about the organization was that there were a lot of rules. A lot. Which at first seemed counter to the idea of *volunteer*. I thought, *Shouldn't they just be happy I'm here at all?*

First was the god-awful uniform: long pants, no jeans, no leggings, nothing too tight. Something like loose khakis are most appropriate. Rubber-soled shoes. No open toes. No bare ankles. A heavy-gauge polo shirt, which for some reason only came in size men's XL. Over that went a navy apron with pockets stuffed with antibacterial wipes and pet hair removal rollers. No jewelry. No perfume. You also wear a giant 1979-style Polaroid camera from a strap around your neck that constantly bangs against your breasts when you walk so you can leave a picture of your dog with the people you visit. The point of such a uniform is to make sure that the dog is the center of attention, not the human. You are not a woman in the Friends on Four Paws uniform. You are not a man. You are simply a sexless Good Samaritan. I got used to it, even embraced it. Maybe it would be good for me to be stripped of all vanity and pride in my appearance.

Second is your bag, which you must carry with you at all times. There is a very precise list of equipment that must be included in your bag. No variations are allowed. Visits are performed in teams—two handlers, each with a dog. One handler is designated as the coach. The coach is the boss. Once you've been volunteering for a while, the designation of coach is arbitrary because often both volunteers have equal experience. In three years, I was never the designated coach, for reasons I don't understand. I was used to being the boss. At work. At home. Even when I was on jury duty, I always ended up as the foreperson. But not once was I listed as coach on my assignments for Friends on Four Paws. I can't say it didn't bug me.

Very often the coaches on our visits would take the position of authority way too seriously, as if they'd done something to deserve the title. They'd do spot checks of my equipment bag, quiz me on Friends on Four Paws policies—obviously these were people who didn't get to be in charge very often, and they were going to make the most of it. They were drunk with power.

One woman named Terri, whom I worked with a lot while visiting at Children's Memorial Hospital downtown, had been suspended from her teaching job for smacking a kid in her classroom. Her hearing in front of the disciplinary board was a year away, so she was in teacher jail with full pay until then. She was always the coach on our visits, and she lorded it over me.

I repeat: she was on probation from teaching for smacking a kid, and I still didn't get to be the coach. And Terri was a real stickler. She wrote me up once because I was missing the required two-foot traffic leash from my bag. I argued that I had never in my three years used the two-foot traffic leash. She countered, "It's on the list. It needs to be in your bag," and reported me on the website. If you get three violations in a year, they kick you out. "That's strike one for you," she declared, not unhappily. I tried to think of it as an exercise in humility: maybe I'm too attached to being in charge.

Lastly, there were the requirements regarding your animal. On the day of your visit, your dog must have been bathed and groomed within a twenty-four-hour period. You had to keep your dog six feet away from the other therapy dog at all times. You may not let your dog so much as greet the other dog at your visit. They are at work; this is no time for play—try explaining that to a Jack Russell terrier.

My dog Cabot is the gentlest giant of a golden retriever that ever lived, but I was frankly shocked when he passed the therapy dog test. He's not really a "pay attention and follow instructions" kind of guy. Sometimes he's not even that well behaved. He mounts strangers and humps them; he pulls on his leash when he sees a squirrel, dragging me helplessly across the park; and he's obsessed with food. But on the day of his exam, he transformed into a model citizen. He passed with flying colors, and when he earned his therapy dog vest, he was proud. He was made for this work.

When he wore the vest, it was like he knew he had a job to do. He tiptoed around the old people, never made a peep when he spied the other dog volunteers, didn't steal food off hospital trays, let the sick kids pull his ears, and even ignored the squirrels in the parking lots.

The final requirement was your visit balance. You must maintain a visit balance of three visits per month. You can do more. You may not do less. Period. Most of the volunteers are retired. Some work part time. I didn't meet any other volunteers who still had children at home. When I started, all three of my kids were still in the house. My career ebbed and flowed, but when it flowed, it gushed. Sometimes three visits a month was extremely challenging.

And that's why I got on the Friends on Four Paws shit list.

I had managed to keep a zero balance, just keeping my head above water with the minimum three visits per month for the three years I'd been in the program. I worked with people who had more than two hundred visits in their account. I didn't even know how that was possible. Were they doing three visits a day, seven days a week? My visit balance had dipped into the negative a few times when I had scripts due or during the kids' soccer seasons, and I had to work like mad to bring my balance just back to zero. There are no excuses for not visiting—not sickness, business, vacations, death—it doesn't matter; the clicker keeps on clicking away. So last year when I was shooting a TV pilot and all of the activities surrounding Dayton's senior year in high school were happening at the same time, I starting getting in arrears, and it snowballed.

And nothing I said to my team leader about extraordinary circumstances seemed to get me any leeway because every time I checked the website, my negative balance continued to grow.

I understand why the policy is there. I'm sure there are a lot of people who like the idea of being a volunteer but flake out when it comes time to make the actual commitment. And they can't have that. You've got sick kids and old people counting on you. You can't have a bunch of ancient and confused people sitting in the lobby of the depressing old folks' home on visiting day, clutching at their cardigans, their rheumy eyes scanning the empty parking lot, asking the nurses over and over, "Where are the dogs? I thought the dogs were coming! Did the dogs forget about us?" But I've been a model volunteer. Except for that one nick on my record for the missing two-foot traffic leash, I've shown up for my visits on time, my dog bathed and groomed, my uniform pressed and standard issue, and my visit materials in order, even in the midst of production and pilot season when the stress of deadlines was waking me up in the middle of the night in a cold sweat, ripping at my nightgown—feeling like someone was trying to drown me. But still, I showed up, driving through rush hour traffic, taking notes on scripts as I made my way to keep my promise to babies and veterans and stressed-out college kids. I kept my visit balance in the positive column for three straight years. But the last six months, it slipped. It went from negative three to negative twelve. Then I had to take Dayton to visit colleges, and it just kept going.

The woman in charge of the program, Joy—a misnomer if ever there was one—called to remind me if it stays in the negative for six months, Cabot and I would be booted out of the program. I asked what I could do to stop the bleeding. Maybe a short leave of absence?

She said they don't give leaves of absence to anyone, ever.

"Ever?" I asked. "Even if someone is juggling a lot more than the average volunteer?"

"What would happen if we made an exception for you?"

"Nothing!" I promised. "Nothing would happen. Except maybe I would stop having a mild panic attack every time I went on the website and saw my name with a sad doggie face next to it and a big negative check mark. I'm not used to being a disappointment to people," I tried to explain. "I grew out of that. I'm a Goody-Two-shoes now. I'm an underachiever who somehow miraculously became an overachiever, and that sad doggie face on my profile page makes me feel I'm slipping back in the other direction. Please, Joy, there's got to be something I can do!"

Finally, Joy, out of the goodness of her heart, offered me a solution. She said she was aware I was a writer and she had been unhappy with the descriptions of the facilities on the website for years now. She offered me this barter: if I would rewrite the facility descriptions, she'd "pay" me one visit for every ninety minutes I spent writing. One visit for ninety minutes of writing? And while I was doing this, I asked, would the negative visits stop accruing?

"Of course not, because . . ." I know. There are no leaves of absence! So let me get this straight: My negative balance was now up to twenty-three. At ninety minutes for each visit, I could write a novel in the time it would take me just to get to negative six. I mean, I *wouldn't* write a novel, but the fact is, I could. I could certainly write more than descriptions of elder care facilities visited by dogs. Not to mention, as I was erasing the negatives that already exist in my account, more negatives would continue to accumulate because I still wouldn't be completing my visits.

It was like one of those nightmares where you had homework to finish, but every time you turned the page more pages would appear.

This was outrageous. I was a professional writer. I was almost indignant to the point of shouting, "Do you have any idea who I am?" Thankfully I stopped short of that.

That would not have been a proud moment. Joy said she completely understood if it was too much for me and it was certainly my choice. She would be sorry to see Cabot and me go, though, since we were two of the most popular volunteers in the program. Wait, what? Popular? With whom? I liked that. Joy said we were one of the most requested teams, which was surprising since we were also the most underachieving.

Underachieving? Popular? I was enraged and flattered and ashamed and confused.

"Well, maybe I could try to write the descriptions," I told her.

"Great," she said. "See how far you get, and if it's too much, let me know."

I agreed it would be worth a try. She said just to write about my experiences at the places I'd visited with Cabot.

I decided to start with my experience at the Silver Palms, a memory care facility in West LA. I would write about Smitty. My visits there were the third Saturday of every month. My regulars, Sue, Nancy, Richard, Smitty, and Vera, were always waiting for me in the lobby. A semicircle of wheelchairs and walkers. They loved spending time with Cabot. And I loved spending time with them. The residents were all in various stages of Alzheimer's and dementia. A visit to Silver Palms was a little bit like the movie *Groundhog Day*.

Cabot would lie on his back while they scratched his tummy and asked the same questions over and over:

"How old is he?"

"Nine."

"Have you had him since he was a pup?"

"I sure have."

"Does he like coming here?"

"He loves it."

"How old is he?"

"Nine."

"Do you think he likes coming here?"

"I do."

"How old is he now?"

Maybe I liked it best because it took the spook out of what lay ahead for me with my own dad's journey into Alzheimer's. I'd been going there for three years, and I'd seen people deteriorate. Many had died. My favorite of all the residents was Smitty, a feisty and funny white-haired flirt. When I first started coming to Silver Palms, Smitty was still pretty sharp. He and his wife, Vera, were in the independent section of Silver Palms, part of the group waiting for me in the lobby. He took great care in his dress—always in a short-sleeved dress shirt with a bow tie and black slacks. His full head of white hair combed. His brown eyes twinkled when he teased his wife, who didn't speak anymore but smiled at Smitty when he squeezed her hand.

When Smitty saw Cabot coming through the lobby, he'd call out his name, like Lou Costello used to call Bud Abbott, in a booming voice: "Cab-ot!" Even when his memory didn't hold much else, he always managed to come up with Cabot's name. When I asked if he wanted me to take a picture of Cabot and him with the giant Polaroid camera, he'd joke that would cost me twenty-five cents—a lot of women were trying to get their hands on pictures of him. One Saturday I came to Silver Palms, and Smitty and Vera were missing from the lobby. I asked some of the other residents if they knew where they were. They didn't know who I was talking about. That's maybe the saving grace of Alzheimer's—when someone goes missing, you forget they were ever there.

When I asked the nurses about them, they told me they'd been moved to the VIP section. The VIP section houses the residents who can't live independently anymore. The access doors are locked with a code to get in so they don't wander. It's more depressing than the main area. Residents shuffle around, some in terribly anxious states. They can't go outside or close the doors to their rooms. I was shocked.

Smitty seemed okay just a few weeks ago. They said it was Vera. She wasn't doing well, and Smitty insisted on going behind the locked doors of VIP with her.

When Vera died, Smitty took it hard. When I visited Smitty, he only talked about Vera and their years together. He asked me if I was married yet. I said, "Not yet, Smitty. But I'm okay. I've got my dog." I didn't want him to know I was divorced. I cared what he thought of me.

He patted my hand and said, "Oh, don't you worry. You wait until someone who deserves you comes along. It'll happen. You're too wonderful to pass up." Then he held my hand for the rest of my visit.

The next two times I visited, Smitty wasn't there. He'd been taken to the hospital. He was failing, and it didn't look good. I thought I'd never see him again. I was surprised when I came a few Saturdays later and Phillip, one of the caretakers, told me Smitty was back from the hospital. They expected that he was going to die anytime now and asked if Cabot and I would go see him in his room.

I took Cabot to Smitty's room. A picture of Smitty and Vera was hanging outside. Smitty, a young man, six foot two in his air force uniform, one of the prized Airedales that he'd told me about so many times, stood next to him. Vera, feisty and pretty, was on his other side, looking up at Smitty with stars in her eyes. I entered the room with Cabot. Smitty was in his bed.

He didn't look like himself. His hair was a mess, and he wasn't wearing his big glasses or his usual pressed short-sleeved dress shirt and slacks, just a rumpled hospital gown. He would hate to be seen like this. He looked small. Above his bed were at least twenty-five Polaroid pictures of Cabot and Smitty that I'd taken from my visits over the years.

I led Cabot over to the bed and called out to Smitty. He was moaning softly. I lifted Cabot up so he was standing and placed his front paws onto the bed so that his head was level with Smitty's. Cabot stayed there, even though it probably hurt his hips; he knew what he was supposed to do. I said, "Hey, Smitty. Look who came to see you. It's your best pal, Cabot. He missed you." I placed my hand on Smitty's cheek and just watched him for a moment. Cabot licked Smitty's forehead, and he opened his eyes.

When Cabot came into focus, Smitty smiled weakly and said, "Cab-ot!" Then he just closed his eyes. I lifted Cabot off the bed. He laid down on the floor next to the bed.

Phillip looked at me. He said, "That's the first time Smitty's talked in two days."

I kissed Smitty's forehead, and then I bent down and kissed Cabot right on his dog lips.

I sent the story to Joy.

An email came back less than thirty minutes later. "Thanks for this, Kari, but try not to make it about you. I'll look forward to reading more."

I wanted to find something that gave me perspective and purpose. Something to keep my feet on the ground in

Hollywood. Well, Friends on Four Paws did that. They stole my looks, my authority, my heart. They don't even like my writing. They brought me to my knees. With nothing else to do, I buckled down and continued my penance. I whittled away at that shameful negative number, but when I was down to a mere minus eleven, the clock ran out. Like a prisoner on death row, out of appeals, my six months in the negative column was up, and Cabot and I were booted out of the program.

Never mind that I had spent 1,260 minutes writing for the organization—rules are rules. And unlike Hollywood, where the rules change depending on who you are, the rules are the same for everyone in Friends on Four Paws. There was something oddly satisfying about that. My last contact with Joy was this: "Kari, please return your materials via FedEx within seven days, or we'll come after you for the cost of replacement. It's been a pleasure working with you. Joy."

Isolationism

Last week I was diagnosed with inflammatory breast cancer. I diagnosed myself by googling the words *unexplained breast bruise*, and there it was. Even though none of the images looked at all like my unexplained breast bruise, I consulted enough blogs to know anything that appears anywhere on the bosom of any shape, color, frequency, or duration is most likely definitely cancer. My results were conclusive: this was the end. Further research on some lady's website who posted pictures of adorable kittens to honor her niece, who succumbed to my disease, told me that IBC is aggressive and largely untreatable, given that by the time it presents itself with any symptoms, it's often too late. "But I just had a mammogram!" I typed into the WebMD message board. Doesn't matter, I was told by Wikipedia. This crazy cancer can't be detected by a mammogram. Which explains why when Hartford Tanbaum, my radiologist, performed not only a mammogram last month but even an ultrasound because of what he called my "dense breasts"—I think he was flirting with me—found nothing.

Dr. Tanbaum reads my mammogram, then squeezes cold jelly on my chest and rubs the ultrasound wand around in it, staring at an incomprehensible gray blob on the screen before announcing everything looks good. Then he uses his hands to palpate my breasts, and he always waits until this moment to ask me how our mutual friend, Allan Rice, is doing. Allan is the son of his good friends, the Rices, and was a writer's assistant on my show, *The New Adventures of Old Christine.*

He's young and smart and delightful, but it makes me feel icky to discuss him with Dr. Tanbaum's hands on my slimy boobs.* Anyway, the whole experience is all very strange—medicine mixed up with work mixed up with nudity—and when I leave, I feel like I did something naughty with Allan Rice and I can't look him in the eye when I get back to the office. But now I'm dying, and none of it matters. I can't believe I've wasted time on meaningless things like watching endless back-to-back episodes of *International House Hunters* and experienced endless back-to-back episodes of road rage.

I called to make an appointment with my internist because it's always good to get a second opinion to the internet. The lady

---

* *My boobs aren't always slimy, by the way. It's from the ultrasound jelly. Usually they're dry as a bone.*

who answered the phone said Dr. Ghim didn't have anything until next week. I told her it was kind of important to see him sooner rather than later, but he was out of town at a breast cancer conference. "Ironic," I said to her with a brave laugh.

She said, "So do you want the appointment next Wednesday or not?" I took it, then got to work googling alternative treatments in Mexico. Just for the record, I'm not a hypochondriac. Except when it comes to cancer.

It's because fifteen years ago when I had vague symptoms and laughingly said to Dr. Ghim, "The internet says I have cancer," he didn't laugh.

Instead, he said, as he was feeling the lump on my thyroid without a smile, "Let's get a biopsy."

"Are you serious?"

He said, "It's probably just a nodule. They almost always are. If it was anything to worry about, I'd be very surprised."

Dr. Ghim did the biopsy and told me I'd have the results in four days. I didn't think about it much; I had three-year-old twins, a six-month-old, and a pilot in production. I didn't have time for drama.

When he called me four days later, I had honestly forgotten about it, but Dr. Ghim sounded upset. "Wow, Kari, I really didn't think this would happen. It's malignant. I'm really surprised."

I told him, "It's okay." Then, "Hey, you thought of the biopsy, so that was good!" Trying to comfort him.

I didn't know what else to say, so Dr. Ghim continued. "We should schedule surgery to remove your thyroid. They'll look at the lymph nodes at that time and see if it's gone there. If it has, those that are involved will have to be removed as well. After surgery, we'll schedule you for radioactive iodine treatment. It's targeted radiation to remove any abnormal cells that have traveled elsewhere in your body. You'll have to stay away from your kids for ten days because you'll be radioactive, and you don't want to expose them to it. Do you have any questions for me?"

I had pulled over to the side of the road so I could process the information, and I said, "I don't think so. Thank you so much." Then, because he'd never actually used the word, I had to ask, "So I have cancer?"

Dr. Ghim said, "Yes, you do, but if you have to have cancer, thyroid is the kind to get." Then he added, "If it came back after surgery and radiation, I'd be really surprised." I wish he hadn't said that thing about "really surprised"—that's what jinxed us the first time.

I sat in the car for a minute, trying to think of who I should call. I couldn't tell my parents. My sister trumped me with her brain tumor, which had recently started to grow again, setting in motion the ticking clock counting down to her demise. And I certainly couldn't tell the network or studio who were producing my pilot—as the sole breadwinner in my family, I couldn't risk shaking their confidence in me. And besides, according to

Dr. Ghim, I had the great kind of cancer. I could handle this on my own. So I scheduled the surgery quickly and quietly.

It was uneventful and seemingly successful, and now I needed to move on to the radioactive iodine portion of my treatment. Ten days away from my babies.

Several of my husband's brothers and their wives volunteered to come to Los Angeles from the East Coast and help him out with the kids. They were very worried about him having to manage everything all by himself. Another brother and his wife, who lived in Los Angeles, thought, "Hey, since everyone's going to be out here, maybe we should have our anniversary party then so everyone can come!"

I reminded them, "Well, I'll be in isolation, so *I* won't be able to . . . Oh. I see. You weren't talking about me." And their party planning began.

I checked into the isolation ward at Cedars in preparation for the radioactive iodine. I was put into a room with glass walls. No one was allowed in or out. I communicated by telephone to the nurses, who could also see me on a monitor at the nurses' station. They passed my meals through a sealed opening in the door, like prison. I would be in there for the first twenty-four hours after I received the radioactive iodine, when I would be unsafe for human contact. When it was time for the treatment, two men appeared at the door to my room. They wore contamination suits: all white, with gloves and booties on their feet, masks covering their mouths and noses, and goggles. One of them held a stainless-steel tray with a small Dixie cup perched on it. The one behind him carried a similar tray with a clear plastic cup of what looked like water. They punched in a code on the keypad of the door leading to my room. It could only be opened from the outside. Which I understood. I could already feel a strange temptation to run out into the hospital postradiation and randomly touch people to see if I could make them glow.

They entered the room like space men, walking awkwardly in their suits. The first man said to me, "I have the radioactive iodine in this cup. It's in two capsules that you are to swallow."

The second man said, regarding his cup, "This is water."

I stared at them. I was wearing a flimsy hospital gown. I could feel the air where my backside was exposed. They couldn't even risk *breathing* in the same room as these capsules, and I was supposed to ingest them? Put them inside my body? Was this really a good idea?

The first man held forward his tray, and I took the Dixie cup and looked inside. The capsules looked regular—they weren't pulsating or anything—so I tipped the cup to my lips and dropped them down my throat. The second man was ready with the water on his tray. I took the clear cup and washed down the radiation. The men put down their trays, then motioned to a third person who had appeared on the other side of the door that they were ready to be let out. And they were gone.

I try really hard not to feel sorry for myself, but this period in my life took me down. Not because of cancer. Or fear of dying. Or even being separated from my babies. This took me down because it was the first time I thought, *Oh, I'm completely alone.* And I knew why. Because *I* did this. No one was here for me because every time someone asked if they could help me, I said, "I got it." I went to work with a fever instead of taking to my bed and letting someone else take over. Not letting anyone bring me soup or even run an errand or, God forbid, do the rewrite without me. And now nobody thinks about me. Because I'm always fine. So here I am, all alone and radioactive. When you take too much pride in your own self-reliance, people stop thinking you have needs. It's the same thing with always paying the check. After a while, people stop reaching for it.

The Chinese say the thyroid is the resentment gland. Well, no shit. I don't think I'm allowed to resent people for not doing what I wouldn't let them do. But I do. But I don't think I'm allowed. But I do.

After the twenty-four hours at Cedars, I was released to go to my beach hotel, which would be my prison for the next nine days—the Casa del Mar in Santa Monica. They gave me pages of instructions about what to do if my urine spilled where it shouldn't. There was a hazmat number to call if I threw up someplace in public. I was in one of the hotel's bungalows with instructions to the staff that I was not to be disturbed and no one was to enter my room. No housekeeping, no room service. I took my isolation seriously. I know a guy who had the same procedure who left his family and went to gamble in Vegas for a week. I said, "What about the people you came in contact with who have kids?"

He said, "They're not *my* kids." See, that's the kind of guy who *should* get cancer.

I have never been so bored in my entire life as I was that week. But at least everything at home was fine. When I called, my in-laws regaled me with stories about what a blast my kids were having without me. Annabel had learned a song on the piano. Elias could throw a curve ball. And Dayton was sleeping through the night. Apparently, *I* was the one holding them back.

Finally, one of my oldest friends braved a visit to me. We sat out on the patio and didn't touch. She talked nonstop about how her kids were driving her crazy—I was so lucky I got to chill at the beach. She ate all of my potato chips and smoked all my cigarettes—yes, picking up smoking again was my morbid reaction to cancer. I guess my friend forgot I couldn't go to the grocery store to replenish my supplies.

Then she apologized for monopolizing the conversation—but she'd been really stressed. This whole thing with me really made her think about her own mortality. Suddenly, she got weepy thinking about how sad it would be if she died and just had to go home and hug her kids. I wanted to unleash a stream of radioactive urine onto her self-obsessed foot. But at least she was there, and from this moment forward, we jokingly referred to her as Florence Nightingale.

I made it through my quarantine without losing my mind, but it gave me a lot of time to think about what I was doing wrong in my life. I arranged the thousands of baby photos I'd taken over the past six years into albums, and as I reminisced, I made a list of things I could do better: better friends, better family. I was so angry with everyone and everything, I was going to give myself cancer again. And maybe now, if my IBC diagnosis was correct, I actually had.

This time, however, I have the chance to do things differently. This time, I wasn't going to be brave. Or stoic. Or resilient. I was going to be a giant, helpless baby. I was going to ask for what I needed. I would whine and demand. Be weak and weepy. Make people drive me places and cook me meals. I might even wear a diaper. I would accept charity and giant favors that I would never repay. I would rely on everybody but myself. I would learn to lean.

But sadly, my doctor disagreed with my diagnosis. My bruise, he said, was probably the result of my recent tumble with a garden shed I moved in the backyard. I was not patient enough to wait for someone to help me, and because it was too heavy for me to move by myself, it tipped over and fell on top of me. Luckily, I was able to get out from under it, or that's how they would have found me.

Which would have been some kind of poetic justice, I guess. "Here lies Kari; all she had to do was ask." It's okay. Someday I would get cancer or some other life-threatening condition. Everybody does. And I would be ready.

Under the Influence

I have recently discovered that personalities don't really exist. Our moods and temperaments are only a reflection of whatever chemicals, hormones, and temperatures are running through our bodies at any given time. My discovery came when I flew to Boston to be with my son Elias after he tore his ACL during a soccer match. It ended his hopes for his soccer season his junior year of college, and he was depressed and scheduled for surgery—expected to be completely incapacitated for at least ten days afterward. Determined to make the best of a bad situation, I sprang into action, renting an apartment close to campus so he wouldn't miss too much school, renting a car and a parking space so I could transport him from surgery to home and physical therapy without relying on taxis or public transportation. I arrived two days before the operation to fill the apartment with all of his favorite foods and treats. I ordered a PlayStation 4 with the latest FIFA game to pass the boring hours and put a smile on his face. I set up an air mattress for myself on the floor of the living room, giving him the bedroom, and splurged for the extra-special Game Ready machine that iced and compressed his leg, providing relief and fast healing next to his bed—the same one the Red Sox use. There was nothing I wouldn't do to speed his recovery and ease his pain.

The day of the operation went smoothly. I sat worried and waiting for over three hours while the orthopedic surgeon bisected his patella tendon and grafted a strong piece of it to his femur and kneecap.

His surgeon, Dr. Anwar, came out and told me he expected Elias to make a good recovery. Once E had woken up from the anesthesia, they came and got me, and I rushed to his bedside. He was groggy and seemed no worse for wear. They armed me with oxycodone to get him through the worst of his pain. The nurse and I gently lifted him into the car, and we made our way back to the apartment at Downtown Crossing, where *my* nursing duties would begin. The first hint of how bad the pain was going to be was on the ride home when he screamed every time the car hit the smallest bump—and this was *with* the nerve block that would wear off in twelve hours.

The next five days were hell. Setting my alarm to deliver the pain medicine every three hours, changing the ice in the Game Ready machine every two hours, adjusting the brace, moving him to the bathroom, fighting with him to eat—we descended into a bad dream. The air mattress I was sleeping on had a leak,

starting out mildly uncomfortable fully inflated, then flatten-
ing into a plastic pancake by morning, leaving me waking up on
the hard wood floor after my two-hour sleep cycle. My patient
was a tyrant, an ogre, an asshole. There was very little I could
do right, from applying the compression stocking—which is like
putting pantyhose on another person's foot, a task I can barely
manage on my own leg and have long since abandoned—to the
way I screwed the top on his water bottle to the food I deliv-
ered to him in bed. When I tried to help him adjust his brace,
he howled in pain and accused me of dropping his leg. If I woke
him up to take his medicine, he snarled at me, "Why did you
wake me up?" And if I didn't, he scolded me: "You didn't wake
me up? Now I'm not going to be able to stay ahead of the pain
like the nurse said!"

When his girlfriend came to sit with him in the afternoons,
he asked me to close the bedroom door in a tone that suggested
I was some nosy neighbor who had a freaky interest in his private business. But since it was still my job to keep him on schedule, visitors or not, when my alarm sounded to change the ice
or deliver medication, I would knock gently on the door, move
in quickly, service my patient, then duck back out, nodding and
apologizing like a mistreated geisha.

Once out of earshot, I would take one of the chair cushions
from a barstool in the kitchen, carry it into the bathroom, and
cry into it so I couldn't be heard until it was time for either a

meal, a pill, or a bathroom run for my ungrateful patient. This was our life. There was no day, no night, no night nurse. The low point: me stealing his prescribed stool softeners because my own lack of sleep, exercise, and love had succeeded in binding my middle section up like a bale of hay. I hated myself for taking his ill temper personally and tried to give myself pep talks when I could escape the apartment to stock up on ice at the CVS across the street. I muttered to myself, "He's in pain. You have to try and remember that," resembling the many homeless people who lived outside our temporary apartment, which, it turns out, wasn't in the best neighborhood. When a man got stabbed and collapsed in the doorway to our building, bystanders watched in shock as I leaned over him to unlock the entryway door, then step over his body to get inside, saying, "Sorry, but I have to get in there. I'm a nurse," which must have added to their horror when I didn't pause to check on the victim. My only concern was that my patient would wake up from his nap and find me gone, in which case there'd be hell to pay.

My son's pain didn't seem to affect his treatment of anyone else. When his dad called to check in, I could hear him falling all over himself with gratitude. "Wow. Thanks so much for calling. I really appreciate it. What? You're sending a card? You don't have to do that. But thanks, Dad. Love you too." I moved in after the phone call ended to hook him up to the continuous passive motion machine—a medieval torture device that bent his leg back and forth to prevent scar tissue and restore his range of motion. He was supposed to be in it twelve hours a day, and I worried he was slacking off. It was not my idea or prescription, but I was met with unmasked hostility when I inquired about how many hours he'd logged. "If you're so worried about it, you time it," he snapped. Not ending with "Love you too," which sent me back to the bathroom to shed my martyr's tears into my crying cushion.

My friend Kathleen has a saying: "Mom is the worst part in the play." And I know this.

It's not like I've been showered with gratitude and over-whelming appreciation before. They're kids. They take things for granted. So why was I devastated? Why did this utter lack of appreciation suddenly feel so intolerable? When Dr. Anwar called to check on his progress, I gently mentioned Elias's sour demeanor. The doctor said, "Oh, sure. That happens when the anesthesia is leaving a person's system sometimes. Also, he's on some pretty strong pain medication. It causes personality changes in some people." As soon as he said it, it made perfect sense. It's chemical. This wasn't my sweet boy. He's not awful and entitled and unkind. But even knowing this didn't help (because I'm the worst nurse ever). I reached out to a friend, feeling guilty and worthless, but she suggested perhaps the explanation for my sudden intolerance of bad treatment and being taken for granted was chemical on my part too.

They say when you are approaching menopause, the flux of hormones and the loss of estrogen can make you a little crazy, which is perhaps why I felt as sensitive as an exposed nerve. My friend suggested this was the time to hold my tongue and give myself a time-out when I felt my emotions getting the best of me. She said, "Just don't react. Remember: your feelings aren't facts." Maybe. But the more I thought about it, the more I came to my own defense. I don't think I am crazy *now*. Is it crazy to want to be treated like a human being? I think the crazy was what came before. And now I have come to my senses. The hormone that was necessary to keep me on task, conceiving, then birthing, then raising three children is leaving my system and I'm waking up. It was the stuff that told me even if I worked a twelve-hour day, I must come home, cook a healthy meal, check the homework, make snacks for the team, and tend to everyone's emotional needs, making sure that selfish interruptions like sleep or personal hygiene didn't get in the way. And thank-yous didn't always come. But I didn't need to be appreciated. My satisfaction was in the doing, the nurturing, the sacrifice. That was the hormone talking.

And now, emerging from the fog of my reproductive years, that wasn't going to work for me anymore. In fact, a lot of things were going to have to change. Like, I'm not driving sixty miles to meet my parents for dinner, I declared to no one, trudging down the wet Boston sidewalk in search of a wine store.

If I'm always the one who pays? I'm never going to be the one who drives. You come to me or starve. Guess what else. Next Christmas? You can forget about me painstakingly choosing only the most thoughtful (yes, expensive) and perfect gifts for everyone, while I'm lucky if I get dollar-store shower gel that makes my chest break out. From now on, we're drawing names. Twenty-five-dollar limit. Christmas is not on me anymore—I'm resigning as Santa Fucking Claus.

Also, my kids *do* have to celebrate my birthday. And I want presents, or I'll go out of town on theirs instead of my usual habit of showering them with the equivalent of a *Price Is Right* showcase.

I don't want to be the bigger person anymore. Or the understanding friend or the good daughter or even the supermom, I think as I'm trudging back from the wine store, head down, three bottles of chardonnay clinking against each other in their plastic bag.

And another thing—I'm suddenly noticing that every man, almost without exception, states his opinion as fact. When I was under the influence, that didn't really bother me—probably because it served some evolutionary purpose, as in "a man with confidence most likely has viable sperm." But now that my mission is no longer about propagating the species, these men just seem like self-important assholes. I'm done with them too.

I feel bad for men, dealing with the new me. They liked it the other way. The martyr, the nurturer, the mommy. But I can't help them. And I think that's why men my age start flocking to younger women around this point. It's not the taut skin or high breasts, although those things are nice; it's the fact that those women are still on the juice.

They can still tolerate him blabbing all through dinner about how hard his job is—even if she has the same job at 60 percent of the pay. I could no longer sit still while he talked about his glory days on the baseball diamond or football field. Or his *band*, for fuck's sake. But she, in her twenties or thirties, could still feign interest, high as a kite on estrogen and eggs as she was. She could cluck over his sore throat and pretend he was good in bed. She liked making him feel better. Making him happy made her happy. It's bad design on someone's part because the men I know are so much more determined to be part of a *we* as they age, just as the women I know want to be left the fuck alone.

These men are as interested in a committed relationship as we women were in our twenties, when they were running for their lives. Cruel.

I tried to explain my theory to Gene the shrink—who happens to be a man in his midfifties—when he called to check on my son and me. He listened carefully, then suggested maybe

I should talk to someone about hormone replacement. "What? Why?" I snapped. "What is it that I need to cure exactly? My liberation? My independence. My clear-eyed revelation?" He wondered out loud if I was depressed. Certainly sleep deprived. "You aren't listening to me! I'm telling you I feel like I just woke up. Like I've been released from indentured servitude!" He wouldn't get on board. Later I realized that maybe Gene was thinking of his own wife. Now that their children are out of the house, was she going to abandon him? Stop taking care of him when he needed her most? He was probably scared—he didn't want to be alone. Pussy. Suddenly I hated Gene too. He had to go.

In retrospect, given my mood, I probably should have canceled my dinner date with the perfectly nice man (a friend of a friend) who'd helped hook us up with our temporary apartment. He'd done nothing to deserve me in my current state, but it seemed too late to cancel, and I could use some good food. My son was feeling better, and his girlfriend was bringing him soup. I showered, but I didn't shave my legs. *Fuck him*, I thought. We went to a fancy restaurant. I was underdressed and didn't care. I answered his questions and told the truth. I didn't laugh at his jokes if I didn't think they were funny. He offered to drive me home, but I said I needed a walk, and that was that.

On my last day, just before my scheduled flight back to LA, I took Eli to his ten-day post-op appointment with his surgeon.

Dr. Anwar was impressed with his progress, the expertise of the bandage application, and the general state of my son. He was even off all the pain meds. The doctor said, "It looks like someone's been taking good care of you."

Elias answered, with tears in his eyes, "I didn't make it easy on her, but my mom is the greatest. I'm so lucky." At that moment, it felt like love itself flooded my bloodstream—endorphins or oxytocin or something—and my heart almost burst. I had to bite the insides of my cheeks to keep from sobbing since I didn't have my crying cushion with me. All was forgiven.

Back at the apartment, Elias asked if I was okay if he went to the dorms to see some of his friends. I said I'd be fine. I just wanted to clean the apartment, stock the refrigerator, and change his sheets before I flew out. "You don't have to do that," he said.

"I do. I have to," I said.

After he'd gone, my phone rang. It was my dinner date. He said he wanted to let me know he had a great time with me.

"*Why*?" I asked, not making a joke.

He laughed and said women are always trying too hard around him. I didn't try at all.

"Well, if you want a woman who doesn't make an effort, I'm your girl."

He asked if he could drive me to the airport. I said he could. I didn't shave my legs.

Something to Believe In

I tried to believe in God in high school. Two of my best friends were super religious, and I wanted what they had: a certain relaxation about life because they had an answer for everything. The world made sense to them, and they were never alone. Believing in something bigger than themselves contained them in a way that I craved, so I tried to connect myself to God. I whispered into the dark, "If you're here, Lord, give me a sign. Doesn't have to be anything big. I just need a little proof." I tried to make it super easy for God. My challenges were simple. "If I wake up sleeping on my left side tomorrow, you exist. If I'm on my back, you're not there." When I was driving, I'd say out loud, "If that stoplight changes to green before I have to hit my brakes, God is real." "If I suddenly have a beautiful singing voice, but only when I'm singing about Jesus, I'll believe." "God, make that cloud pass in front of the sun now . . . Now. Now. Okay, now." But God never accepted any of my challenges. I stayed flat on my back until morning, the stoplight never went in my favor, and even though when I joined the choir at the Pomona First Baptist Church, I thought I sounded pretty good singing about Jesus, the Christian next to me started putting her hand over the ear facing me whenever it was time for my second soprano verse, as if my lack of tone was throwing her whole game.

When I went away to Lutheran confirmation camp, I asked the pastor, who described his belief in God as "solid as the earth and sure as the sun that rises each day."

"Just tell me how you *know* it's true. What happened that made you believe?"

His answer: "Nothing happened. I know because it's what my heart tells me. That's what faith is. You can't ask God to prove himself to you."

"Why not? He did all those things in the Bible to get people on board. Why did dead people stop coming back to life or turning into pillars of salt? Why did donkeys stop talking and frogs stop falling from the sky and seas stop parting as soon as the Bible was finished? Don't you think that's a little suspicious?"

The pastor thought I was a smartass and stopped calling on me when I raised my hand. All I was asking for was one story about a night in his youth where a voice whispered in his ear, "There's a fire. You must get out."

And he saved his whole family, hence, his faith in God. How about a near death experience? I would have taken a potato with the face of Mary. But there was no story. At least not one he was willing to share with me. "Just believe it because I say so," which is what I got from every believer I'd ever questioned, and that seemed like too much to ask, so I eventually gave up on God.

Next, I started looking for *someone* to believe in, but people are a disappointment, especially when you're expecting them to magically fill your life with meaning and purpose. *Especially* especially when you date actors. One particularly ill-equipped guy whom I decided I loved—a short, bald drama student with the intensity of Brando, according to himself—told me he couldn't get serious because when he got famous, he wanted to be free to fuck Daryl Hannah. I continued to love him even though he provided none of the things I was seeking, and our last moment together was me lying on the floor, sobbing, "You don't love me enough."

His response was, "No one possibly could." Men were not going to be my salvation either.

My uncertainty turned to superstition the older I got. Without faith to keep the world safe and with an ever-expanding knowledge of how many bad things could really happen to myself and the people I cared about, I started knocking on wood and honking in tunnels—thinking if I did these things, I would be successful, planes wouldn't crash, my children would stay off drugs. When a hair on my arm grew longer than the others, I decided it was my lucky hair, and as long as I left it alone, all would be well. I wasn't insane. I knew it wasn't true. Well, I knew it *probably* wasn't true, but on the very remote chance that it was, I let it stay.

And how is my lucky hair any crazier than the nutty things other people believe? People sprinkle water on babies' heads to keep them from eternal damnation and don't put a milk glass in with a plate from a roast beef sandwich to keep souls from getting contaminated. I can have a lucky hair. I understand why people cling to their nonsense: if you don't believe in something bigger than yourself, life and death are just dumb luck, which means anything can happen at any time to anyone, and there's just no comfort in that.

Then, finally, when my sister, Lisa, died, I wanted to believe in ghosts. At the end, when her brain tumor had won and she'd stopped being Lisa, I'd sit on her bed, hold her hand, and tell her, "I want you to haunt me. Okay? But if you can, do it in a nonscary way. Like, don't show up behind me in a mirror. Try doing it during the day."

Lisa was thirteen months older than me, and she'd already haunted me in life. She was a perfect student, never earning less than an A from kindergarten through college.

She was valedictorian, magna cum laude, president of things, chairwoman of others—she was a force. When I'd walk into a classroom the year behind Lisa, a teacher's face would light up. "Lisa Lizer's sister!"

I was sorry to disappoint them, but they soon learned I was going to be a different experience for them. I took Algebra One twice and Spanish One twice; I dropped out of geometry and barely went to class my junior and senior years at all. I had a full-time job at Pup 'N' Taco and drove to commercial auditions in Hollywood on a regular basis. I forged an excuse note from my parents about three days of every week, and I think the school was as happy as I was not to have me there because no one really asked any questions.

After Lisa died, I stayed vigilant, trying to feel if she was with me from the other side. I got hooked on the TV show with John Edward—not the politician, the psychic medium who claimed to communicate with the dead. His show was called *Crossing Over with John Edward,* and it was on right about the same time I was crawling into bed with my dog and coffee mug of chardonnay. There were two back-to-back episodes on five days a week, and I became obsessed. I got it into my head that my sister was going to send me a message through John Edward, and I had to pay attention. He worked with a studio audience and called out random images, pictures that flashed in his mind, until someone in the audience connected to what he was saying and they'd raise their hand. He'd say, "There's a police officer. I'm getting a *G* name."

A woman's hand shot up—they got her a microphone. The woman tearfully said, "My father, Gary, was a police officer."

John would continue to make sure they were talking about the right guy. "I'm seeing a short illness. Nobody thought he was going to die from it. Even his doctors."

The woman nods frantically. "Yes! That's Dad!"

John continues: "He says you were all in the room when he passed."

The woman, starting to sob, says, "We brought him his favorite black-and-white cookies from the deli. And he went into cardiac arrest."

John says, "He wants you to know that he had a bigger problem than the doctors realized. It was nobody's fault. Nobody is to blame. He's making me feel like this is very important. No one is to blame. Does that make sense to you?"

The woman can barely breathe. "We filed a civil suit against the hospital." The studio audience gasps. So do I. But this message wasn't for me.

Weeks went by with dozens of episodes and not a word from Lisa. Then, one night, as I was about to put the sleep timer on, John Edward said, "I don't know why, but they're showing me that episode of *Will & Grace* where Grace gets the water bra." I sat up in bed. I was writing for *Will & Grace* at the time.

"Is that you, Lisa?"

No one in the audience was connecting to what John Edward was saying except me. He went on to describe the episode further until one man finally raised his hand because he thought his mother had a cousin named Grace, but I knew Lisa was trying to tell me something.

The next day at work, I told another writer, Jhoni, about the episode. Because she was a good friend, she agreed that it sounded like my sister. We needed to get in touch with John Edward. When we called the number at the end of the show, we got a recording that said John Edward was booked up for the next two years, both for private and group readings and even audience tickets for his show.

I would have probably given up there, but Jhoni tracked down the number of the production company and called in her official capacity as the executive producer of *Will & Grace*. She left a message for John saying that we were interested in using him as a guest star on the show and asking him to please give us a call back. Her phone rang within five minutes; it was John Edward. Jhoni flattered him and flirted with him and asked if he was, by any chance, going to be in Los Angeles anytime soon. She'd love to get together with him and talk about his part on the show. He said he was coming to LA the following week to do some talk shows, but his time was all spoken for. He said he'd call her if something opened up. I still wasn't sure how we were going to scam him into connecting me with my deceased sister under these false pretenses, but Jhoni felt confident, so I was hopeful.

The next week, we didn't hear from John. Jhoni tried calling him again through his production company, but her messages weren't returned. On Friday, I was picking up the kids from school when Jhoni called my cell. "You need to get to West Hollywood right away. One of John Edward's appearances canceled, and he has a couple of hours before he goes to the airport. He said he'd meet you." I was wearing slippers and sweatpants—school pickup line attire because I didn't have to get out of my car. Jhoni was insistent that I didn't have time to go home and change. I asked another one of the moms, who was waiting in line for her kid, if my kids could go home with her for an emergency play date. She loaded my kids into her car, and I headed over the hill to the hotel where my medium was staying.

It was a classy, small boutique hotel on a quiet side street in West Hollywood. I had instructions to go straight through the lobby to the elevators and go up to the fourth floor, and if the privacy sign was on the door to his room, I shouldn't knock, just wait—it meant John Edward was still with the person he was reading before me. Outside his room, the privacy sign was on the door, so I went into the stairwell and waited. I could hear muffled voices through the wall but couldn't make out any words.

I silently whispered a little prayer to Lisa to please talk to John Edward. I asked her to say something really specific so I would know it's her. After about twenty minutes, I could hear the hotel room door open and John Edward saying goodbye to a man and a woman. As soon as I was sure they were gone, I came out of the stairwell and knocked on John Edward's door, where the privacy sign had been removed. A moment later, he opened the door.

It was weird. This man who had been putting me to bed every night was now standing in front of me. John Edward is from Long Island. He's very tan, with very white teeth and product in his slicked-back hair. He wears tight sweaters to show off his big muscles. He's exactly the guy I would dance with and inevitably make out with in clubs the year and a half I lived in New York. The waitresses I worked with at the Comedy Cellar in the Village questioned my "bridge and tunnel taste," but my attractions were formed when I saw *Saturday Night Fever* more than twenty times in high school—that movie really worked for me. John Edward was even a former professional ballroom dancer.

I only mention these things because everything about John Edward makes him the most unlikely psychic medium you've ever met. It's also part of my answer when people ask if I think he's a charlatan. In order for someone to pull off what would be such a monumentally complicated and cruel scam on each person that he reads, either privately, on his show, or during his national sold-out tours—to pick up their body language, to study every twitch of each person's eye, probably do some kind of background check when he had access to a name and dig up information to produce as a psychic "hit," to exploit people's grief for his own gain, this guy would have to be some kind of evil genius. John Edward is warm, engaging, funny, adorable. Definitely not evil. And—I say this with love—not a genius. He's just a dude.

I tell him Jhoni is coming, too, but she's going to wait for me on the roof by the pool. She'll come say hello when we're done and, you know, talk about his part on the show. He didn't seem particularly anxious about that, which was a relief to me, though in the back of my mind, I couldn't help but think, *If he's psychic, why doesn't he know that Jhoni and I are kind of running our own scam?*

John Edward and I sit across from each other, and he asks me if I got there early. I tell him I've been sitting in the stairwell for about twenty minutes. He smiles and says that there was a very bossy person who came through in his last session—*came through* meaning from the other side, the dead side—that his last client didn't recognize. It must have been for me. This person was very strong, wanted to do things her way, didn't want to wait.

I smiled and said, "I think I know who that is." *Sounds like my sister, the chairwoman,* I thought, but didn't tell him. I was still interested in testing him—and didn't want to give him too much to go on.

He asked, "Who's the young male that passed? An *A* name?"

"I don't know," I told him.

"Yes, you do," he said. "The bossy one says you do. She really wants you to know the young male with the *A* name is with her."

"Well, I really don't think I know a young male with an *A* name."

"Yes, you do," he tells me confidently.

John Edward paused at this point and seemed to be gathering information from the great beyond, then continued. "This bossy person is not really above you. She's not in charge, in spite of what she thinks. You know how kids say, 'You're not the boss of me'? That's what I'm getting. Is this your sister?"

I confirmed with a nod, suddenly afraid to speak and scare the moment or the ghosts away. Then things started moving fast. Bits of information. Snapshots of random things, some of them specific, some of them not. He talked about Lisa's children and said Lisa was grateful for the woman with the *P* name for taking care of them. *Their aunt Patty*, I think. He tells me Lisa says she sees her daughter in church. I didn't know Kady went to church, but when I ask later, I find out that she goes regularly. He talked about Lisa's last days with details of the hospice room and the nightgown I bought her. And about every ten minutes, he'd say Lisa was insisting again that I know the young male who is with her. The one with the *A* name. I don't know. "Yes, you do," John Edward and my sister continue to insist.

At one point he started talking about someone whom my sister was bringing through. A man who had taken his own life. I was confused at first; then I gasped, "I think that's Jhoni's brother! Should I go get her?" He told me to go. I ran up the three flights of stairs to the roof and found Jhoni, who was sitting in the shade, reading a script. "Jhoni, your brother's here!" Jhoni jumped up and ran back down the stairs with me, grilling me about how it was going. Did I talk to my sister? "I think so," I told her. "I don't know. It's crazy. You'll see."

Back in John Edward's room, Jhoni listened as John Edward gave her images supplied by her dead brother, brought to West Hollywood by my dead sister, channeled by a medium whom we'd conned into seeing us by offering him a part on *our* TV show because I thought my sister was talking to me on *his* TV show. It was strange. It was soothing. And while it wasn't like having our siblings in the room, it was something.

My sister finally pushed Jhoni's brother back through the spirit door, and Jhoni went back up to the pool. I stayed in that room for more than two hours. My sister never gave up on the young male with her, and her frustration with me was growing.

I should clarify. Growing up, my sister and I weren't the best of friends. We were mean to each other. I lived to torture her. She had a bad temper, and it was too easy and too funny to get her to go ballistic. When she brought her boyfriend home from college, the man she would later marry, the only thing I knew about him was that he was Native American and she really liked him and I was not to embarrass her. She introduced Jim. "Jim, this is my sister, Kari."

I raised my hand and said, "How." You know, old-fashioned Indian style. My sister instantly punched me right in the stomach. I fell to the ground, gasping for air. I know it was obnoxious and ultimately painful, but it was completely worth it.

Now, I could feel my sister's ghost's impatience growing. If she were here, she would no doubt be calling me an idiot. "I don't know any young dead male with an *A* name!" I whined, as if I were actually fighting with Lisa instead of my medium.

Then John Edward had a flash. "Oh. What's buried in the backyard?"

I thought for a minute and then remembered. "Alfie!" The hamster that died last week when he was only four months old. John Edward laughed, saying that was a first, but my sister wasn't about to let it go. That sounded right. She was a pain in the ass.

We did end up using John Edward on *Will & Grace*. Mostly because he was so kind and generous and funny but also because I don't think it would have been smart to fuck over a person who is potentially connected to all the dead people who ever walked the earth. Another thing that confirmed his legit status: he was not a good actor.

A few years later, I heard from him again. He called my cell phone one day. "Hi, Kari, it's John Edward. I'm just checking in. Sorry if this is weird, but these past few days, I keep thinking about you. Someone's putting you in my head. Are you okay?"

I told him I wasn't. My brother had died a few days before. His drug addiction had finally stopped his heart. John told me when he was taking a shower that morning, I came into his mind and he just kept getting the message for me, "I'm sorry, I'm sorry, I'm sorry." He thought he should tell me.

John Edward came to visit me a few weeks later in LA. I was doing *The New Adventures of Old Christine* at Warner Bros., and he was as warm and regular as he'd been a few years before. He told me that he'd been going through some stuff. Trying to figure out how to take what he does and make it have an impact on people's lives moving forward. He didn't want just to be a link to the past or a carnival act—I don't remember if those were his words, but that was the idea. Then he sat with me and told me the picture he was getting from my dead people on the other side was the image of a french drain. You know, when you dig a trench around your house to channel water away from the building to protect the foundation from damage? He said in every family there are cycles of pain and dysfunction that get passed down, creating more pain and dysfunction—like water running down a hillside.

He told me that what he was being shown was that I was protecting my children from the runoff by redirecting the energy, changing the direction, breaking the cycle. My sister could see it. My brother could see it. Probably my grandparents and aunts and uncles and dead hamster could see it. It was my reason at a time when I couldn't pick out a reason for anything. John Edward gave me a huge gift. Say what you want about psychics and magic and ghosts—John Edward finally gave me something to believe in.

#NotMe

I'm sorry. I'm not a joiner. I know for most people, aligning themselves with like-minded individuals brings comfort, makes them feel like they belong. But for me, it makes me feel less special. I wouldn't be caught dead in a sorority or church group. I've never been part of a squad, team, or troop. I don't read books in clubs or take vacations on buses. If I could sing, I'd be a solo act. I could have no doubt benefitted from an Al-Anon meeting or two along the way, but the idea of standing around bonding over like traumas, then holding hands and singing "Kumbaya" or whatever is my idea of a nightmare. I like to believe that my problems are uniquely my own. I don't want people to relate to me. It doesn't help me for someone to say, "I've been there," or "I feel you." I like to believe that you don't "feel" me. I have made a perfectly satisfactory lifetime of failed relationships from being misunderstood.

There are those women who seem to like coming together over collective experiences in a different way than men. I was never one of those girls. The ones who openly cried together or marked their cycles on calendars. Girls who shrieked when they discovered things they had in common. "Me tooooo!" they squealed when they realized a mutual love of baked brie or Scott Baio. "Oh my God. Me. Too."

Maybe because growing up, the women in my family didn't share personal feelings or intimate information. I learned how to use a tampon by reading the back of the box. A box that I stole from my mother's sweater drawer, where she hid them from the view of my father and brothers. I stole from her, she replenished, and it was never discussed. I don't know where my sister got her tampons. It was just some shameful secret underground tampon railroad that worked for the womenfolk of the family. It's the same drawer where the paperback copy of *Jaws* was stashed, which was the only explicit sexual information I received—specifically the scene on the beach before the girl skinny-dips in the ocean and becomes the shark's first meal. That was all the material I had to work with until Maria Stewart told me about blowjobs, and both pieces of data were traumatic and, I hoped to God, fictional. My father's *Playboy* magazines, on the other hand, were kept in plain sight next to the toilet in the hall bathroom. The men in my family also openly farted and made no apologies for forgetting to flush the toilet or gaping boxer shorts—all sending a loud and clear message to elementary school me: it's different for men.

In the early 1980s, I worked as a waitress at the Comedy Cellar in the Village in New York. This is the same place where Louis CK recently made his unapologetic comeback to stand-up comedy. The restaurant upstairs from where the comics performed served Middle Eastern food on chalkboard tables that customers scribbled on while they waited for their falafels. It stayed open until 4:00 a.m., at which time the waitresses—all women—began scrubbing down the tables with steel wool and Ajax until all the chalk dust had been removed. Management was a little fussy about this.

You were required to have them come inspect your tables before you could clock out, and if they had even the slightest chalky film, you were sent back to do it again before you were released into predawn New York City with your less than twenty dollars in tips, deciding whether to brave the creepy subway home or spend all of your tip cash on a safer taxi ride, picking the shards of steel wool from under your fingernails, hair smelling like shawarma grease. Management was also convinced the waitresses were stealing food, so they installed a camera in the dessert fridge. Which was deeply insulting, even though, yes, every time someone ordered a piece of cheesecake, I would shave off just a little sliver for myself and quickly shove it into my mouth before delivering the slightly undersized remainder to my customers. It was just a little sliver. It was really good cheesecake. It felt like a harmless offense, but they were serious.

If they caught a waitress taking even a bite of something she hadn't paid for, she was to be terminated, no questions asked. The Comedy Cellar didn't fool around. Unless, apparently, you were a comic who liked to drop his drawers and masturbate in front of young women who would lose their source of income if they made a fuss. In that case, all you had to do was lay low for ten months, then come back to the stage to pick up where you left off. Nobody really cared about the women he held hostage with his penis power play. Because he's famous. And he's funny. And he's a man.

When he returned to the stage, the audience sipped their drinks and ate their hummus and undertipped their waitresses and, I heard, gave him a standing ovation. Comics also get their cheesecake comped. It's different for men.

As a comedy writer, most of my success came at a network where there were rumors that the president liked to assert his dominance by exiting his private bathroom in his office midmeeting minus his pants to show his penis to unsuspecting women who hadn't asked to see it. I don't know why this is a thing. Most people don't like looking at a penis. They do it because they're in love . . . or they think the guy's funny or they like the way he plays the guitar. But being surprised by a penis is like being surprised by a slug in your slippers. This is a strictly male move. Some men like to let you know they have power—in large and small ways. The insecure ones like big trucks and tiny women. They stop sleeping with you when you're fat or when you're old or when you're more successful than they are. Money makes them feel powerful. And guns. And killing things like bunnies and ducks. I can't fathom showing my vagina unbidden to anyone. In fact, I'm hard-pressed to display it to people who have asked to look at it. I mean, I know a vagina is not a penis. You can't whip it out, for one thing. It doesn't whip, completely eliminating the "ta-da" factor. And masturbating in front of anyone is inconceivable, since I can't even masturbate with my dog watching. And even if I could physically manage any of those things, I can't imagine it would result in a long and successful career at the top of my field. A lady who touches herself at business meetings doesn't go far. Even in Hollywood. It's different for men.

I work in rooms that have traditionally been dominated by males, and the message was always clear: "Be a good sport, and we'll let you stay." If a woman in a comedy room objects to a joke made at the expense of her dignity, she is invariably met with "Oh, come on; I thought you were a comedy writer," implying that her being offended means she has no sense of humor. So a woman has two choices: laugh along or be held up as an example—"See? Women aren't funny." I don't blame the men. We're ruining their fun. And that wasn't the deal. We promised to keep our shit in the sweater drawer.

As all of these things have unfolded, my brush with the players and places has evolved into a sordid game of six degrees of separation from yuck. It's forcing me to ask myself if not being a joiner has somehow made me complicit. I had always really hoped success was its own revenge. Then came Dr. Christine Blasey Ford. As I watched her telling her story, brave and alone, something changed for me. Because I believed her. Because I've been where she's been. I know what she knows. I've been held to the bed. I've been laughed at, ridiculed, shut down. And as I watched, all I kept thinking was that I'd bet after her long day of reliving her adolescent nightmare and apologizing for being traumatized, she'd get back to her hotel or home or wherever she goes, and someone would still ask her, "What's for dinner?" Because men still want us to take care of them even when they so blatantly and cruelly show they have no intention of taking care of us. Even the good ones just aren't getting it. Because it's different for women. I'm not a joiner, but joining has been thrust upon me. So in support and sisterhood, I'll step into the circle, become one among many, order the T-shirt, learn the secret handshake, and declare kumbaya, motherfuckers. Me too.

Tick

I walked into Everlast Home, where my father is cared for, with Fred, my wirehaired wiener dog tucked under my arm. When I was admitted through the locked and alarmed door to the Alzheimer's wing, called Wisteria, Shirley intercepted me two steps into the room, hunched over in her wheelchair, tied in with a bed sheet. "Do you have your gun?" she asked me, in her gravelly voice that sounded like a gangster dame from an old black-and-white movie.

"Am I going to need it?"

"Well, the police sure aren't doing anything about it, and the bodies are lining up like ducks in a row," she informed me. Shirley's trapped in a reality that is as dramatic as it is consistent. And we are all players in her play: guests at a weekend wedding, stuck in the hotel where her family members are being murdered at an alarming rate. I accidently smile, and Shirley tells me I wouldn't think it was so funny if it was my relatives being murdered, that's for sure. She spins away from me and moves quickly across the room, moving her wheelchair by shuffling her fuzzy-slippered feet along the linoleum floor, begging every resident and caregiver to help her save her family before another one dies. The caregivers have been listening to it all day and are weary.

They wave her off. "Shirley, nobody's dead."

Or they just ignore her altogether and continue their conversations with each other about their kids or their weekend plans, how their husbands are pissing them off, or which diet is working for them at the moment.

Almost all are fairly overweight. They cart in their Weight Watchers meals from home but never skip the industrial sheet cake served to the residents after lunch.

I'm amazed by their hearty appetites. The smells of the place alone put me off food for the rest of the day—the way the soaked-diaper urine odor settles into my nostrils for hours after I leave. It has me sniffing my shirt sleeves all the way home, sure that I rested my arm in something because I'm getting such a strong whiff of piss it makes me feel like I'm drowning in it. But the kind of women who care for other people's aging parents are stronger than me. They are not sensitive to smells. Or sounds. Or sights. Misery. Tragedy. Despair. Even death. They braid each other's hair with the same hands that wipe an old man's ass, cut the crust off someone's grandma's fungus-y toenail, then dive into their lunch box for a protein bar even though breakfast was just half an hour ago and it's supposed to be their midafternoon snack. Their warmth, laughter, and nonchalance in the face of my father's deterioration can sometimes feel like a relief on the hard days and sometimes feel like an insult on the harder days. A couple of the women have been there too long. Like Sondra, who snaps at the more difficult residents and handles them too roughly when she guides them back to their chairs after lunch. Verna's hooting sounds get right under her skin, and I can see her thumbs pressing into Verna's bony arms with their crepey, mottled skin as she hisses between her teeth to shut up and sit down or she's going to go back to her room for the afternoon.

Dorian is my dad's favorite. She's the only one who can get him to eat. She never gets frustrated. Just smiles and flirts and asks him questions while sneaking in bites of mushy chicken casserole between laughing at his jokes.

I think she genuinely likes my father, which makes me genuinely like her. I don't think any of them like me all that much. I think they would prefer I didn't hang out for so long. My empty house and downtime from work has left me with the hours to settle in for long afternoons. I'm sure they prefer to do their work unwatched. They used to offer me bottles of water and ask me how my drive out was, but they don't anymore. I think they think I've gotten too comfortable there.

The other residents get mixed up in Shirley's drama sometimes in whatever way their own reality can make sense of it.

Reba is always certain she should be somewhere doing something, if only she could remember what that something was. She's skinny as a stick because of her constant motion, doing laps around the large room crowded with pleather recliners all facing the large television set that always seems to be playing either *Grumpy Old Men* or that Charlie Sheen movie where he's a baseball player. Reba only wants to help and spends most of her days moving from one resident to the next, adjusting their clothing, fussing with their hair, rolling up their pant legs—getting shooed away, scolded, and, a lot of times, kicked. Reba tells Shirley she would be happy to get some laundry together or even bathe the dogs for the parade tomorrow if that were something she was interested in. Shirley snaps back at Reba, "What the hell are you talking about? Parade? There's no parade! These people are dead! What good is a parade when your family has been killed?" Reba gets her feelings hurt and goes to pout over in the corner, where Jim, the resident perv, sees an opportunity to go comfort her by sitting too close and resting his hand in her crotch.

I find my dad on the other side of the room, in his recliner, half asleep, his San Diego Chargers blanket folded across his lap. He's not paying any attention to the weekend wedding hotel murder mystery or anything else.

"Hey, Pop, look who came to see you!" I say, loud enough to startle him awake.

He opens his eyes, and when he sees Fred, he smiles. "Well, hey! I wondered where you were! Where's he been?"

I set Fred on his lap and tell him I had to take Fred home for a bath. My dad asks where Fred lives. I say he lives with me in Sherman Oaks. My dad looks confused. I tell him it's okay. "We're here now. Don't worry about it." My dad asks what I'm going to do. "Nothing, Pop. I came to sit with you. Is that okay?" I pull up a chair but inspect it for anything gross before I sit down. I'll stay here for the next three hours or so, while he naps and eats lunch and pets Fred. I set Fred on his lap, and he immediately burrows under my dad's arm, all the way up to his armpit. Such a good dog.

My dad worries that dogs aren't allowed at this place and we're going to get in trouble if we're caught. I'm not sure what he thinks "this place" is, and I ask him. "The barracks," he tells me.

"Oh," I say. "Well, I got a special pass for the day." I tell him Fred is a therapy dog and I got permission from the . . . general. That seems to satisfy his worry. He's become a real stickler for the rules and order, always worrying about doing the right thing and not stepping on anyone's toes. It's quite a shift from the hell-raiser I grew up with. The dad who tied my bicycle to the back of his motorcycle on our camping trip to the desert and dragged me full speed over the trails until we hit an unfortunate bump and my bike went flying one way, my body the other.

The bruise that resulted from the top of my shoulder to the back of my knees was a secret to be kept from my mother. And it earned me a ten-speed bike.

When I tell Gene the shrink about the hours I spend at Everlast, he's alarmed. He says the shifting reality of the place would cause him great anxiety. I tell him it doesn't really bother me at all. Strangely, I feel equipped to handle it.

It even feels familiar to me. It's like being in an interactive play or an extended improvisation, and if you follow the basic rules of "Yes and . . ." and stay away from "No, actually . . ." it can even be kind of entertaining. Like game night. Gene doesn't like game nights. But for me, these days at Everlast are an opportunity to surrender. At Everlast there is no time or place. For Shirley it's 1974. Reba is in Barstow, getting ready for the Fourth of July festivities. My dad is stationed at Camp Pendleton.

The first very noticeable sign of my father's Alzheimer's for me was his growing inability to keep track of the seasons. I'd phone home in the summer from my vacation in Vermont, and he'd ask how much snow was on the ground. We'd talk about the twins being away at college and when they were expected to come home next, and he'd "remember" they'd just been home for Thanksgiving last week, even though we were having our discussion in June. His orientation of time was slipping away from him. *My* first noticeable trouble keeping track of time started when my third and final kid left for college. I decided that would also be a good time to take a six-month hiatus from work. It would be a nice chance to be alone with my thoughts, creatively regroup, and consider what this next chapter might hold for me. Big mistake. Without the kids and without work, I was adrift. All the things that gave my life structure were suddenly gone, and without them, I had no sense of time or place.

My life used to be a pie. A pie that divided into slices—the school year and summer were one way the slices divided.

Youth soccer seasons and Little League were other pieces of the pie that divided the year into sections. When the kids started playing club sports and the soccer became year-round fun, that didn't have the same effect, but there were still other markers in place that let me know where I stood, timewise, and how far I had to go to get where I needed to be. I could bribe with these markers: "Don't start slacking off now. We're only two weeks away from winter break, and you get three weeks of vacation!" And for the bigger milestones, the years kept track of how far we had to go: "Three more and you'll be in high school. How did that happen?" "Just one more and you get to drive." "This time next year, you'll be in college." Work had seasons too. Summer was the time to pitch new ideas, fall was the time to write, spring was production, and then you start again.

But now nothing means anything. In California, there aren't even seasons to divide the meaningless hours, days, and months into segments to clue me in. Monday is no different from Saturday when you don't have a student or a job. Six a.m. is the same as 6:00 p.m. or 3:00 a.m. when you have no place to be. There isn't anyone who needs to be picked up. Or dropped off. There are no segments. It's all one big time. One ceaseless tick without a tock. I have to think for a minute—is it spring or summer or fall? Am I supposed to be Christmas shopping or planting a garden? There is no back-to-school prep. No summer camp registration. I have gone from having an extraordinary number of things to do to having an extraordinary amount of free time. If your life is not spoken for by any calendar or clock, it's not that hard to see how one could slip away, wondering finally if anything or anyone really exists at all.

Happy Endings

It was the Friday before Mother's Day in what was a particularly brutal year for me. My marriage ended and my sister died, simultaneously. And both of their deaths were painful and slow. I was writing for *Will & Grace* during the worst of it, and Jhoni helped see me through with so much generosity and humor that I swear I think she saved me. She decided I needed a special treat this Mother's Day. "I've booked you a massage with this outrageous Russian. His name is Vlad, and he'll give you the best massage you've ever had in your life." I protested that I couldn't leave the kids with a babysitter—my guilt was already at a maximum. But she said, "No, he comes to you. Put the kids in front of a video and take it. You can do one thing for yourself." Maybe she was right. I'd spent the last six months driving back and forth between San Diego and LA, commuting between failing my sister and failing my kids, coming to terms with each five-hour round trip that life is too short to tolerate unhappiness. Maybe I could use a neck rub.

Vlad showed up fifteen minutes early wearing a white V-neck T-shirt tucked into white pants with a black belt. He was tall, with dark curly hair, a flat nose, and a broad chest. You would cast him as an orderly in a 1950s psychiatric hospital or an attendant at a sanitarium in *Doctor Zhivago*. I had the kids stashed in my bedroom. The twins were six, and Dayton was three. I had provided snacks, water, and entertainment.

I ordered them on my bed and told them in my most serious and hopefully feared mom voice, "Do not come out there. You are not to move off this bed, and I mean it. Not for toys, not for tattling, not for anything. Seriously, unless this room is on fire, you will not leave it—you got me?" They were already transfixed by the *SpongeBob SquarePants* video I put in for them, so I was pretty sure I could count on them to stay put for sixty minutes. I hoped so because I couldn't imagine what their small brains would do with the sight of their mother, naked on a table, lubed up and being rubbed down by a large Russian man. I only knew the sight of my father by the pool that day, when I was ten, rubbing suntan oil into Ginger Reagan's already brown skin, then her turning over and saying, "Aren't you going to do the front?" has stuck with me for over forty years. She was my best friend's mom and my mom's best friend—my first lesson in "There's always stuff going on you don't want to know about."

When I got back to the family room, Vlad had assembled his massage table and placed two sheets on top with one pulled back. He'd also lowered the lights and lit the candle I had on the coffee table. He told me he'd go into the hall bath to wash his hands while I got undressed and slipped between the two sheets, facedown. He was quiet, respectful, and serious, like a doctor about to go into surgery. I took off my clothes, super quick—I didn't want him coming out of the bathroom and catching me half undressed. I didn't know where to put my bra and underwear. It would seem way too intimate if they were just lying on the couch in full view while he worked—also my bra and underwear weren't fit for company. I was in the habit of wearing my three-year-old maternity underpants since no one was going to see them anyway and they were so damn comfortable. And my poor old bra looked like someone had used it in a drunken fraternity tug of war.

I shoved my shameful underthings between the couch cushions and slipped my body between the sheets. Lying facedown on breasts is not ideal. In fact, I've considered designing a massage table equipped with cutout holes that one's breasts could hang through. But I haven't done it yet. I scooched around to find the best possible distribution of my flattened boobs; then I heard the bathroom door open and Vlad call out, in his thick Russian accent, "Kari? Are you ready for me?" I said I was, and Vlad came out, wearing a small apron around his waist that kept his unscented massage oil at the ready, like a holster. Vlad cracked his knuckles, took a cleansing breath, and pulled back the top sheet to reveal my neglected upper torso, with my tweaked neck and pinched scapula.

I was regretting the twice-weekly stops at Jack in the Box at the Sand Canyon exit on my way to my sister—crispy chicken tenders, ranch dressing in the cup holder, and a supersized Diet Coke—that had become my ritual. Because now my back must look enormous. I said, "My neck and shoulders are in pretty rough shape, so maybe not too deep."

He said, "Vlad is like KGB—I *know*."

He poured oil into his huge, rough hands and placed them on my shoulder blades. The feel of his man hands on my bare skin made me try to think back to the last time I'd been touched and I couldn't come up with it, and suddenly I felt so sorry for myself that giant tears dropped from my eyes to the floor, some of them hitting Vlad's black Rockports that I was staring at through the face cradle. I took deep breaths to push the feelings away. Vlad moved his hands across my upper back, and there was a popcorn-popping sound as every vertebra in my spine cracked.

I laughed involuntarily, which thankfully scared away my tears, and Vlad went to work. Jhoni was right. He was fucking amazing.

He untangled my shoulders in such a pleasure/pain perfect combination of palms, fingers, and elbows that I stopped thinking about my kids in the other room, my fat back, or how I would explain to my husband why our temporary separation had to be permanent. That watching someone die young suddenly makes you ask the question, "If I knew I didn't have time, would I still be doing this?" It makes you realize you have to quit stupid jobs, worthless friendships, and even so-so marriages. You take what time you have to seek out happiness and treat yourself to it. I moaned. I dozed off. I drooled.

In what felt like a minute but was actually forty-five, Vlad leaned down and whispered in my ear, "Kari? Can you turn over, please?" I rolled over onto my back, not caring that the sheet half fell off my body—but Vlad was quick to catch it and replace it gently over my parts, protecting my modesty. Then he reached for my feet. My excruciatingly ticklish feet that have never been touched by human hands other than my own, unless you wanted to get kicked in the face. But somehow, when Vlad held them and started with exactly the right amount of pressure, it didn't tickle—it felt like heaven. Like I could die, and it would be okay as long as Vlad kept rubbing my feet. After a while, his hands started to knead their way upward, pushing on my ankles, then my calves. The muscles released under his touch, and I thought I might fall asleep again. There wasn't a place on my body that didn't feel better in Vlad's hands.

He was past my knees, and with a giant hand on each leg, he started moving up my thighs, his thumbs pressing on the inside while his fingers worked my quads. Jesus.

Vlad said quietly, "Are you okay, Kari?" I said yes, my voice husky and dreamy from my deep relaxation. He kept moving up my thighs, and about every two inches he would ask again, "Are you okay, Kari?" I kept saying yes. He was still moving north, and, boy, he was getting way up there. His hands were now under the sheet and still traveling. At this point a little bell went off in my brain, but I told the bell to shut up because this felt amazing. And he just kept coming until finally his thumbs were resting at the very top of my thighs, on either side of my vagina. He paused and asked again, "Are you still okay, Kari?"

All right, yes, I was slightly alarmed. Yes, my children were fifteen yards away, watching cartoons. Yes, this man was a large, foreign stranger inside my house with his thumbs half an inch from my sex. But Jhoni knew this guy. Did she know about this? Did she pay extra? I thought about the stories from writers' rooms, from writers who, according to most of them, had massages at some point with happy endings like it was no big deal. So maybe it was no big deal. But none of those people were mothers. Which instantly made me mad. Why shouldn't I do what feels nice? Everybody else always does exactly what they want all the time; why do I always have to be the good one? I didn't want to be good. I wanted to be pleasured by Vlad.

I was starved for human contact and tired of taking care of everyone else. And that's why I told Vlad, "I'm still fine, sir." So he pressed on, continuing to work the area, not yet making direct contact but so dangerously close I could barely breathe and it was all I could do not to start humping his hands. It wasn't sex. Or even foreplay. It was performed like a service, like therapy, and Vlad was clearly a professional therapist.

His fingers started moving faster and I thought, *I'm actually doing this! I can't wait to go to work tomorrow and tell everyone.*

That's the thing about a writers' room that's not just full of the same old white men—when you mix it up, with women and gay people, the dynamic changes—more tears, fewer boundaries. We shared everything in that room, and everything was fair game. Those who got hurt feelings or took themselves too seriously didn't last long. When I tried to explain it to people who weren't there, they'd say, "That sounds awful. And mean." And it was. But it was also healing and hilarious. There were eating disorders and anger issues. We all started getting colonics at the same guy's house in Marina del Rey. We drank Red Bull and vodka on show night when we got to the act break. We made bets at the Golden Globes on who could get the most movie stars to touch them. I won when Bono sat on my lap, and for the rest of the season, the white board in the bungalow proclaimed, "Kari got mono from Bono." This was not your father's writers' room. I loved these people. Most of the time. And they loved me. Most of the time. They would understand what was happening with Vlad. And they would tell me it was okay.

But then Vlad stopped before he really got down to business. His hands rested lightly on my pelvic bones for a moment, then went away. I didn't dare open my eyes, but I immediately thought, *Is he getting a knife? Taking a picture? Oh shit. Well, Kari, this is what you get for trying to be open-minded.*

Then Vlad said, "Kari, I know what you need, but I think you'll be upset after." What? Oh no! Goddamn it, Vlad. Of course I would be upset after. Really upset. And deeply ashamed.

I spend three days replaying a conversation in my head where I think I said something stupid to a friend I ran into in the grocery store.

I'm pretty sure I'm going to revisit the moment when I let a stranger get me off ten feet from where I frost my babies' birthday cakes!

No doubt it would have been one of those moments that caused the kind of flashbacks that sneak up on you in your car and cause you to cringe and cry out involuntarily at a stoplight, "Oh God, no!" making you blush to your knees. And Vlad knew it. He really *was* like the KGB.

I said, "Yeah. You're probably right. It's not a great idea." Vlad tenderly placed the sheet back over me and moved to my head, where he began massaging my scalp without saying a word. The tears came again. I didn't want to be divorced. Or sad. Or left alone with my parents.

Vlad reached down and massaged my breasts. I think he felt sorry for me, so he decided to throw me a bone. Then the hour was over, and Vlad disappeared back into the bathroom so I could get dressed. He left me oily, stuffed up, and totally exposed—I was still under the sheet, but, you know, emotionally. When Vlad left, I went into my bedroom, where my kids had fallen asleep in my bed. Instead of waking them up, I crawled in beside them and fell asleep myself.

My cell phone started ringing at about ten—the caller ID said Vladimir Shernov. I didn't answer. He tried back three times, never leaving a message. Probably worried that I was going to report him to the police. Or Jhoni. Or maybe he was just checking on me.

The next day at work, I told Jhoni what happened, and she was pissed. "He's never once fucking tried that with me, and I would totally go for it." Then, "Honey, that's a good Mother's Day."

I asked her please not to make this a "room story" because, you know, you bring things to the room when you're ready to laugh about it. And I didn't have a happy ending yet.

Kate Middleton's Bangs

All day I've been resisting the impulse to click the headline on my AOL newspaper, "What Has the Duchess Done to Her Do?" I call my homepage the newspaper sarcastically, of course, because AOL doesn't really provide any news. If I wanted to know what was happening with the conflict in Syria or the fallout on the economy from Brexit, for example, I'd have to scroll past larger, more important issues like "Blake Lively Seen Shopping Sans Wedding Band" and "Jennifer Aniston Glows in Mexico—Have Her Baby Dreams Finally Come True?"

People make fun of me for continuing to subscribe to AOL. What those people don't realize is that if you try to ridicule me in an effort to convince me to make choices that you deem "hipper," I will dig in. So now enough people have raised eyebrows at my AOL email address that I predict I will die with it. But when this morning's headline tried to entice me into reading about Kate Middleton's apparent hair debacle, I decided to ignore it. And then two screens later, when it shouted to me,

"The Duchess Goes Goth in Scotland!" I didn't bite. But finally, when I was reading a story about home remedies for heartburn, and a banner appeared beneath it that simply said, "BANGS" in bold capital letters with a mysterious picture of the back of Kate Middleton's head, I was pissed. Pissed because, first of all, who gives a shit? And second of all, I did. I hated myself for wanting so desperately to see how Kate looked in bangs. Bangs are always a mistake.

They're good for about a day, and then you have three months of growing them out, vowing never to bang again. But that wasn't the point. The point was Kate Middleton is a highly educated woman, graduating from the same university that my own daughter proudly attended. Kate Middleton performs charity work, championing causes from children's mental health to animal conservation to AIDS research. She's the mother of three children under seven years old and keeps an exhausting travel and social schedule as a goodwill ambassador for the Crown, but the only newsworthy attribute worth mentioning today is her "shocking" new hairdo.

Her husband, Prince William, was in Scotland with her. Not to be unkind, but I assume there were some shocking things to report about his hair as well. The wind on the coast of Scotland is not ideal for a man in his hair-challenged position. If one has only a thin flap covering their royal scalp, the Scottish winds have a tendency to lift that flap in one solid piece, making it appear as if it's about to become airborne—not a good look. Were there reports or headlines about what was going on with the prince's locks? No. When we hear about the prince, it's usually about his heroic helicopter exploits, prowess on the polo field, diplomatic trips abroad. Because those things matter. We don't care about the inch taken off above his collar by the royal barber. We also don't care if he wore the same tie to two events four weeks apart. Is he supposed to get a new tie every time he leaves the house? Of course not. We don't track his weight. We don't zoom in on his skin to inspect the size of his pores and theorize about his skin care routine. We don't assume or inquire if he has snits with celebrities. We've never heard of him "flying into a jealous rage" over Brad Pitt.

And because of that disparity, I decided I would not click on Kate Middleton's bangs. I decided to stage a mini-revolt and refuse to objectify a princess. She is more than her looks, and I'm not going to participate in the culture that reduces accomplished women to their body parts. I just don't have it in me anymore after the tearing down of the most accomplished political candidate we've ever had in this country who also happened to be a woman—the months of scrutiny over her hair, face, voice, clothes—it knocked the stuffing out of me. So I exited my AOL newspaper and walked away, but when I got to the office and opened my computer, it was still there under "Top News Stories."

The other headline shrieked, "Caitlyn Jenner Rocks Hervé Leger Bandage Dress in New York!" So you wanted to be a woman, Bruce? Okay. There will be no more talk of your astounding athleticism, your awards, or your contribution to the world of sports or anywhere else. We are now entitled to pick you apart one new boob at a time. It will feel great when you "rock it!" and less so when the press declares a fashion "miss." We will be watching to see how you age, how you dress, and who you fuck. We will be ready to pounce if your dress doesn't flatter your figure or your figure doesn't hold up through the ravages of time, stress, and trends. I turned off my computer and decided to write on a yellow legal pad for the day. I find myself retreating more and more from technology. Soon I'll be curled in my bed, next to a small burning candle, melting like the liberal snowflake that I am.

Being a girl has always hurt my feelings. I never was a good show pony. Getting dressed up is the worst sort of punishment for me.

In elementary school it actually was my punishment for a bad spelling test or misbehavior—my mom made me wear a dress to school. Acting may seem like an odd career choice for someone who doesn't like to be looked at, but there are people who act to be seen and those who act to disappear. I was the latter. The wardrobe fitting was the bane of my existence. People looking me up and down, frowning at the many ways my body was letting down their hopes for the clothes they bought. Then the producers tromping in, talking in full voice about how they were going to make this work—*this* being me, a human. It really was such a relief when I stopped acting and moved over to the other side of the room. Though not less painful.

These days I find myself sitting on the casting couch with those same executives, directors, and producers when a Truly Beautiful Forty-Five-Year-Old Actress walks through the door for her audition. She's nervous. I try to convey to her with my eyes that I'm on her team. I'm her safe person. She does her thing, and she is barely out the door before it starts. She's been famous since her midtwenties, so unfortunately for her, everyone gets to compare her beauty now to her beauty then. They get to. She asked for it.

"She's getting a little chunky," says the producer with the heart attack body to my left.

"She used to be hot," says the gross bald one with the skin tag on his neck that makes me want to heave up my breakfast bran muffin.

"Her agent swore to me she was holding up," says the casting director as she stuffs the last piece of bagel into her Juvéderm-ed mouth.

"I'd still fuck her," says the studio president with breath that smells like a combination of sausage and sour milk.

Then the rest of the homunculi agree: they'd still fuck her too.

Imagine how relieved Truly Beautiful Forty-Five-Year-Old Actress would be to hear that. I wonder if I should run after her and give her the good news.

"Hey! Hold up! You didn't get the part, but the whole room would still be willing to fuck you!"

Actresses suffer, but no woman escapes it. I'm not imagining it. I worked with a male writing partner for the first time last year and noticed the difference when we'd walk into a meeting. The first order of business was always the unwanted assessment of all things me: "Kari, is that a new shirt? And your hair is shorter. Are you going blonder? I remember when you used to wear clogs all the time. You look like you're losing weight. Are you dating someone? Have you always worn glasses? Your butt looks good in those jeans." I look over to my writing partner—a man my same age—in his rumpled button-down that I think he's been wearing for three days and Levi's jeans. He's peacefully sipping his Starbucks and looking over our script.

Once I said, "Are we going to do him now?" Nobody knew what I was talking about. "What do you think? Fatter? Skinnier? Hair longer? Shorter? Frizzier? What do you guys think about the way Bill's ass is looking these days?"

The executives in the room looked at me, horrified. "Don't embarrass Bill!" they said protectively, as if I were some sort of monster. People don't like it when women call them on their bullshit—in TV they call those women *strident*.

I don't want you to think I'm some kind of feminist hero for not looking at Kate Middleton's bangs. I'm not. I'm susceptible to all the same things everyone else is. And I live in Los Angeles, where the booby traps are everywhere.

Not long ago, a friend recommended a medi-spa in Studio City. A medi-spa is a place that offers beauty treatments but also has some kind of medical personnel on hand to deliver more aggressive treatments that require hypodermic needles and IV solutions. She said there was a woman there who gave the best oxygen facials—just the thing tired winter skin needed. I had tired winter skin. I had tired winter everything. Low-grade postelection depression for sure. So I made an appointment for a pick-me-up facial.

Dr. M, the stylish, foreign-born cosmetologist (a gastroen-terologist in her own country) took one look at my face and neck under the magnifying mirror and deducted, "You don't use sunscreen, eh?"

"Well, I do, but only starting about five years ago, when it was probably too late. My mother didn't believe in skin cancer. And I've spent my whole life outside: at the beach, on a horse, on the sidelines of soccer fields and baseball diamonds and campgrounds."

"Why?" she asked.

I didn't know how to answer that.

Then Dr. M poked at the furrow between my eyebrows with her fingernail.

"You need Botox here. You look angry."

"I am angry," I said. "No Botox, thanks. That's not really for me."

"No Botox? Don't be a baby. I escaped Iran with a five-year-old tucked under my arm, bullets whizzing past my head."

"I'm not a baby," I said. "I'm a feminist."

"A feminist," she practically spat back at me. "What's feminine about your face falling into your soup?"

"I didn't say feminine—"

"No," she agreed.

I gave up. I didn't have to explain myself to this bully.

"Okay, fine. But you should do the nonsurgical facelift. You watch Dr. Oz? He loves it. It's the only thing that really works according to him. Here. Look."

Before I could object, she grabbed a large photo album from the counter and placed it in my lap. Then she announced she was going to mix some ingredients for my facial and she would be back. She left the room. She also left a magnifying mirror pointed at my face so that I was staring at an enlarged fisheye version of myself. That was mean. I quickly looked away and down at the photo album. I opened it and started looking at the pictures, large before-and-after photos of women of all ages. And what I was looking at was a book of miracles. Forty-five-year-old women with turkey-like wattles suddenly had firm jawlines and smooth necks. Sixty-year-old women with soft, jowly faces whose cheekbones had reappeared from beneath the saggy flesh. Seventy-five-year-old women whose youthful glow had reemerged as if by magic. By the time Dr. M came back into the room, I was a believer.

I said, "I mean, these pictures are real, right?"

"Of course they're real. I'm a doctor. I took them myself." Which would have made sense if she were a photographer, but I didn't say so.

"Okay," I said, "I want a nonsurgical facelift!"

"No," she said. "If you're only going to do one, forget it. You might as well not do any at all. You need a series of five to do any good."

God, she was a bully. I agreed to the series of five without even asking how much they cost because I was hypnotized by the before/after magic and also very, very afraid of Dr. M. Turns out I could have purchased a decent used car for what I paid to have my miracle treatments.

She spread the numbing cream on my face and let it work for about thirty minutes while she told me about all the procedures she did to herself. She asked me to guess how old she was. I had no idea. Honestly, it was impossible to tell. She could have been seventy or forty-five. Her waxy complexion looked neither young nor old. Alive nor dead. Finally she said, "Sixty-two." It wasn't impressive or disappointing. Like I said, she just looked weird. So why was I letting her do shit to my face? Excellent question. She fired up the nonsurgical facelift machine and went to work. Several crazy sharp molten hot needles pierced my skin.

"Ow! That really fucking hurts! I thought I was supposed to be numb."

"I do it to myself without any numbing at all. But I also ran from bullets speeding past my head when I escaped Iran."

I know! You told me! I thought but didn't say out loud because I was scared and she was holding a weapon.

After that I didn't dare even wince when she punctured my face with the torture device. I tried to remember my Lamaze breathing from childbirth.

After my series of five nonsurgical facelifts, I can honestly report that I look exactly the same as when I started. Except that I was quite allergic to the numbing cream and developed an ugly rash on my neck. Which I fully deserved because I fell for that sexist Iranian bully's tricks.

The other thing I fell for was the relentless coverage of the duchess's hairdo because when I got back home from work that day, I did it. I clicked on the Kate Middleton story. And there they were. The bangs. You couldn't really even call them bangs. They were more of a feathered fringe. From the urgency of the headlines I'd expected something dire—a shocking, too short, New York–coffeehouse sort of trim. The kind not meant to flatter the face but instead say, "This is what I look like—deal with it." Kate Middleton's bangs were so subtle that her banged self was completely indistinguishable from her former unbanged self. I was tricked into expecting a full-on bang controversy, and they got me. I was ashamed of myself.

Then that click sent me down a rabbit hole of related stories in columns to the left of Kate Middleton's bangs because of whatever woman-bashing algorithm I had unleashed. An ad popped up to sell me a peel that promised to rid me of the hideous uneven skin tone that plagued my disgusting, deteriorating face. Another for diaper underwear for women who pee when they laugh. Horrid pictures of celebrities caught without their makeup that were supposed to make us all feel better about ourselves. I think they wanted Goldie Hawn to kill herself for having the audacity to wear a bathing suit in her late sixties. I finally shut down my computer. My revolution had failed.

Then, as my final act, just before bed, I stood over my sink in the bathroom, my hair combed down over my eyes. I took the scissors from the drawer, and with a steady hand, I did it.

I cut my bangs. I think I'll like having bangs. I like the way they frame my face. I like the way they cover the angry furrow between my eyebrows that's deepened since they didn't elect that woman. I think they look good. I just hope everyone else likes them too.

Late Bloomer

Life is a long and winding road. When I was in the eighth grade, I entered the competition to give the speech at graduation for my middle school. I basically just copied the lyrics to that Beatles song. When I didn't get selected, I was outraged. It went to some overachiever Goody-Two-shoes straight-A student who babbled on and on about being your own person and following your dreams, which is basically the boring way of saying, "Life is a long and winding road." That was pretty much the last time I stuck my neck out for any academic pursuit. I'm a sore loser. Which is unfortunate because as the long and winding road continued, so did my losing streak.

Next up was high school, where I noticed that some girls are born to be teenagers. Like Tina Little, with her Farrah Fawcett hair; square, white teeth; skin that stayed tan all year long; and shiny leg skin that glistened on Fridays when the cheerleaders got to wear their uniforms to school for game days. I tried out for cheerleading, but I was terrible. I have oddly tight hamstrings and a problem remembering dance steps for more than five seconds. It's the same when I cook from a recipe. I have to constantly keep looking at the cookbook—none of the directions stick in my head. So instead, I tried to impress boys by offering to eat anything anybody dared me to: the macho nachos from Del Taco, two Bob's Big Boy double cheeseburgers, four jumbo bags of Peanut M&M's . . . seriously, I can stick my whole fist in my mouth—there's a picture of me doing it in the yearbook.

It didn't have quite the same effect on the guys as a seventeen-year-old beauty queen bouncing on the sidelines, kicking her leg over her head and showing the crowd her skimpy dance pants. Very few teenage boys appreciate funny girls—except the drama nerds.

Another thing the girls in high school liked to do is wear their boyfriends' varsity football jackets. The jackets were giant on them, so the girls felt petite and birdlike. Their hands didn't reach the ends of the sleeves, making them appear shrunken, and for some reason, handless mini-women equaled sexy. The drama nerds were mostly slight bird boys themselves, so their jackets wouldn't zip over my boobs, creating more of a stuffed sausage effect. The only exception was Kevin Wilson, who wore a cape, but wearing the lead from Chino High School's production of *Sing Ho for a Prince*'s cape wasn't really the same thing as a varsity football jacket, so I didn't come into my own in high school either.

In my early twenties, I was a struggling actress, with the emphasis on struggle. Between my infrequent acting jobs, I was a nanny, a housekeeper, a terrible waitress at a comedy club, a terrible waitress at a Middle Eastern restaurant, and a pretty good hostess at a couple of bad Mexican restaurants, including Baja Cantina in Malibu, where my duties included pouring Larry Hagman from his barstool into a cab at the end of the night. I was an elderly companion, a paid party guest, a house-painter, a dog walker, the person who picked lobsters out of a tank in a bathing suit, and a personal assistant to a has-been pervert producer. He wasn't a has-been pervert—he was still a pervert. He was a has-been producer who stood behind me stroking his Oscar—meaning Academy Award, not a nickname for his penis (though I wouldn't be surprised)—while I called Musso & Frank, trying to get him a table for lunch—him insisting he had a regular booth, the person on the other end of the phone having no idea who he was. I told him I had to go home at lunch and let my dog out one day, and I never returned. He called me every day for about two weeks, first threatening me if I violated my confidentiality agreement, then asking if we could talk, finally offering me a raise and a trip to Cabo if I'd come back and keep him company.

After a stint with a pathologically lying boyfriend who pretended to have cancer to get me to have sex with him and not ask too many questions when he disappeared for days at a time,

I took what I thought was a step up and started dating an actor whose star was on the rise. His star didn't have far to travel: born in San Diego, educated at USC, weekends spent either at his parents' beach house or aboard their sailboat venturing up the California coast—the guy hadn't known a lot of hardship. Which was nothing against him. He was just used to fun. And winning. Which is fun. And I was in a low period.

The brakes had just gone out on my car, so I was stringing together odd jobs that were within biking distance of my Venice apartment and praying for auditions that were within biking distance of my Venice apartment. I hitchhiked a few times but only accepted rides from women or men with surfboards on their cars—I don't know why I thought surfers weren't capable of murder. It didn't help that for Christmas my family thought it would be funny if everyone got me a live animal as a gift. My parents got me two cats. My sister got me a rat from the science lab at her college. My brother got me a cockatiel. I already had a dog.

When I returned home from a long, hard day of making fourteen dollars, my pets would all come flying, running, or slinking from wherever they'd been hiding to greet me. It was crazy but kind of magical. I don't know why they didn't eat each other.

The people we hung out with were the young Hollywood up-and-comers who were acting in movies of the week about eating disorders and starting theater companies that gave their profits to Farm Aid. I was a late bloomer in a crowd of early peakers, and I couldn't keep up. I also couldn't afford to skip off to "this amazing spa in the desert" for the weekend. Or even a day at Disneyland. When they'd plan their fun outings and my *soon-to-be-famous boyfriend* knew I couldn't afford to go, he would ask, "Would you rather I stay home with you?" in the same tone of voice I used when I asked my grandma with emphysema if she wanted me to come visit her and her oxygen tank for the weekend. I usually let him off the hook because I think he tried to be a good guy. He even gave me therapy for Christmas. I had to explain to him I wasn't crazy, just poor.

"Why do you cry all the time?" he wanted to know.

"Because it's sad to be poor!" I told him.

It wasn't long before I could tell my *soon-to-be-famous boyfriend* was cooling on me. He didn't think I was that funny anymore, and my constant life dramas were bringing him down. I think he thought dating me would be exotic, like dating a coal miner, but he didn't enjoy knowing about my car problems and nuzzling up to hair that smelled like happy hour taquitos. The reason I knew this is because I read his diary one weekend when he was off gallivanting with the Breakfast Club. Yes, I did. And what I read in that diary was that he was gracefully trying to get rid of me so he could take up with the costar of the movie he had just started rehearsals for.

No, what I read in that diary was this: "I wish I could run away with *soon-to-be-famous actress* and just go to a mountain cabin and stay there forever." It was a long time before I stopped wishing that he and *soon-to-be-famous actress* would be found mauled by bears in a cabin in Lake Arrowhead.

Listen, I know. I shouldn't have read his diary. That was wrong. A diary is private, and that was a violation. No good can ever come from reading another person's diary. I also know that if fifty-year-old me was there, she would have placed her arm around twenty-one-year-old me's pitiful shoulder and walked her gently away saying, "Hey, Kari. Why do you want to be with a person who doesn't want to be with you? Come on. Let's get out of here. You're not a terrible person. You make some really bad choices, but you'll grow out of that. Eventually. Embarrassingly late. But it *will* happen." But fifty-year-old me wasn't there. The only person who was there was twenty-one-year-old *likely-never-to-be-famous me,* so instead of walking away from *soon-to-be-famous boyfriend,* who no longer wanted to be with *likely-never-to-be-famous me,* I came up with a really solid plan. I saw a shirt on a rack outside a groovy Venice clothing boutique, and twenty-one-year-old *likely-never-to-be-famous me* thought, *Hey. If I buy that shirt and I look really great in it, maybe* soon-to-be-famous boyfriend *will like me again!* Oof.

It was pink velvet, with gold and silver paint splashed across the front, Jackson Pollock style. The neck was oversized so that it would casually fall off one shoulder, like *Flashdance*—this was the 1980s, after all. And I decided that piece of clothing would help me belong. The price was $110, more than I'd ever spent on a piece of clothing in my life.

Everything I owned came from a thrift store, and I had a feeling that was exactly my problem. I stuck out like a sore thumb in that group of winners, and my *soon-to-be-famous boyfriend* needed to believe I was one of them. And to be one of them, I either needed to get famous really fast—which seemed like a long shot, even though Larry Hagman promised to introduce me to his agent—or at the very least, I needed to dress like one of them. If I had this shirt, this fantastic and stylish shirt, it would elevate me to the fantastic and stylish level of the people I was keeping company with; it would be the beginning of my own upward spiral. So I spent $110 of my rent, rat, bird, dog, and cat food money on my new prized possession.

That night I rode my bike slowly over to his house, so as not to sweat. I took a moment to run my fingers through my too-blonde hair and positioned the shirt so that it was hanging off my shoulder, hoping to create the illusion that "I'm such a waif, I can't keep clothes from falling off my body" (shrunken bird women never go out of style). Living at the beach and spending all that time on my bike would eventually give me squamous cell carcinoma behind my left ear, but at twenty-one, it just left me with an unnaturally awesome tan. Tight white jeans and low white Converse All Stars—I believe I probably peaked physically that night. I rang his doorbell. My *soon-to-be-famous boyfriend* opened the door, took a beat staring at me, then laughed out loud. "Oh my God. Who threw up on your shirt?"

I sucked in my breath, and then, because I couldn't do anything else, I laughed too. "I know. Isn't it funny?" I had to think fast, so I said, "I made it. Today. Art therapy."

Then he really laughed hard. "You made that ugly thing? You're insane," he said.

And then he kissed me. And I thought, *Hey. I'll take it.* Ask any comedian. Laughs are almost as good as love.

I hung on for another few weeks, but when a friend accidentally revealed that I lied about making the ugly paint-splattered shirt, *soon-to-be-famous boyfriend* used that as the excuse for breaking up with me. He gave me a very high-minded speech about not tolerating dishonesty. He said it as though there was a camera on him and this was his Oscar moment. He was noble and self-righteous. Sure, I fibbed about a shirt; he was cheating on me with his costar, and I could have busted him on it. I would have been well within my rights to scream, "How dare you lecture me about dishonesty when you're plotting your mountain cabin escape with *soon-to-be-famous actress,* you lying sack of shit!" But I didn't. I let him be better than me. I let him walk away believing in the character he cast himself as.

I was tired of trying to fit into that group anyway. All that fake laughing was exhausting. I wasn't even sure I really liked any of them. I don't think I even liked *soon-to-be-famous boyfriend* all that much. And the fake orgasms were killing me. I think I was getting vocal nodes from my performances. But at twenty-one, I was only concerned with whether people liked *me*, not the other way around. Thankfully, I grew out of that. Eventually. Embarrassingly late. I was an embarrassingly late bloomer, which at the time seemed like a terrible tragedy to me. Until now, in my fiftysomethings, when a lot of people are spending time looking in their rearview mirror. I think at the rate I'm going, I should be coming into my own right around sixty, so I'm nothing but grateful.

The road to ninth grade is long and winding, fellow graduates. It's a road littered with stop signs and potholes and tears.

That would have been a great speech.

Inked

I recently decided the time was right to get a second tattoo. I got my first one when I was younger, at fifty years old. I don't know why I started inking myself up in my fifties; I never had the urge to do anything particularly daring when I was actually young. I was never the person to dye my hair pink or pierce my nose or sport a Mohawk. My previous rebellions were limited to smoking cigarettes and dating unemployed people.

My first tattoo happened in Las Vegas. I was taking my daughter, Annabel, and a few friends to a Maroon 5 concert for her fifteenth birthday at the Palms Hotel. I didn't want to venture too far away while the girls were inside, given the unsavory atmosphere outside the concert. There were the usual casino riffraff, people smoking while hooked up to their oxygen tanks, desperate make-out sessions on the seats in front of the video poker machines. I thought maybe I would just have some dinner, but the Palms was also home to the Playboy Club, and for me, the combo of Playboy bunnies being leered at by horny old men and all-you-could-eat sushi left me without an appetite. I didn't dare drink. I needed to stay vigilant in the event that I had to run to the rescue of my innocent young charges. I don't like to gamble—it feels like setting money on fire, and I've never seen the fun in that. So I wandered around the perimeter of the casino looking for something, anything, to entertain me for the next three hours.

I first stopped in to a psychic who charged me fifty dollars to read my palm. She said my boyfriend and I would soon enter a more serious phase of our relationship and my career would take me to a new city where I would make friends easily.

I certainly hoped she was right about my boyfriend and me; since he didn't exist, it was definitely time to take things to the next level. As far as my career taking me to that new city, that was going to be a hassle with the three kids in school, but maybe my boyfriend could help scope out some good schools in the area since I was going to be busy with all my new friends. Before I left, she warned me to double up on my birth control— she saw an unwanted pregnancy in the very near future. The drunk at the Wheel of Fortune slot machine could have predicted my future better than that lady, given my sweaty palms from my premenopausal hot flash and the fact that I was wearing my "nice sweatshirt"—both pretty reliable indicators that I was nobody's girlfriend and rampant fertility wasn't really my issue.

Next door to the psychic was a tattoo parlor. I stopped at the window and surveyed the choices of tattoos available. Then, even though I'd never in my life had the slightest interest in a tattoo, I walked inside and asked the young guy sitting at the counter if he could tattoo a peace sign on the inside of my wrist that looked like I'd drawn it on myself with a ballpoint pen.

"Why?" he asked.

"When I was in junior high, I used to draw one on every morning before I went to school, and I told people it was a real tattoo. I think it would be kind of funny to actually have a tattoo that looked like that, you know?"

"No," he said, obviously not a fan of irony. Or me.

"Well, could you do it?"

"If you want," he said, as if it were the dumbest request any-one had ever made.

Which was a little interesting, considering the guy had a huge Super Mario covering his right bicep. He told me to fill out the paperwork and he would be able to do it in about thirty minutes. While I was filling out my paperwork, initialing that I understood all the ways in which my tattoo could lead to my death, I eavesdropped on a grungy-looking dude in his early twenties who was perfecting the design for the abstract grid that was going to be inked onto his scrotum. I'm not kidding. He was still unsure whether it would look better placed as a square or tilted so it was oriented more diamondesque if you were looking at it straight on. I couldn't help it; I had to give him my two cents. I blurted that square or diamond, there was never going to be a person that thought his scrotum looked beautiful, tattooed or not, with the exception of his mother, because she loved all things about him, and I guaranteed if she knew what he was about to do to the sacred space that was carrying her future grandchildren, she would be horrified. My opinion was not appreciated. My tattoo artist quickly rushed over and got going on my peace sign just to get me the hell out of there. As he began, I quickly asked, "If I don't like it, it's pretty easy to get these things lasered off these days, right?"

My guy said, "If you're already talking about getting it lasered off, maybe you shouldn't be doing it." But too late. My peace sign took all of about twenty seconds, after which he spread some antibacterial goo on it, wrapped it in Saran wrap, and told me to stay out of Jacuzzis for three weeks. I walked back out into the casino, feeling like a new woman, rubbing the Saran wrap that covered the mark that was so specifically my own.

I never regretted that silly little tattoo. I rub it for good luck, and I like the story that goes with it. Most people don't even notice that it's there.

But a lot has happened since then. And while that tattoo was a lark, the one I'm contemplating now is coming from a place of restless discontent. A need to make myself known. The world has changed since my dopey little peace sign, and I don't feel like keeping quiet or unseen. With this tattoo I must decide upon the word, picture, or symbol I want to show the world that represents what I'm all about. And it's important because it's forever. So I started looking on Pinterest to see who I am. I entered the search term *female empowerment tattoos*. The most obvious things came up: fists in the air, girl power with various spellings, encased in everything from candy hearts to lightning bolts. There were boxing gloves, bloody daggers, and more than anything else, the word *pussy* worked into a variety of designs and symbols. I have just recently embraced the word *pussy*—an ironic consequence to a man's grotesque abuse of the word that created a backlash where we all took the word back for ourselves. So now that I've made peace with *pussy*, I don't want to subject it to a future where it will someday morph into a greenish-black blob like the Marine Corps tattoo on my dad's forearm. I'd like to give her a brighter future than that. Also, even though this is an angry time, I have to believe it will pass. It has to. It can't be sustained. So it feels right to place something hopeful on my body. I want my tattoo to represent my positivity in the world. So I *re*-searched, adding the words *gentle, positive, female empowerment tattoos*. This time I got images that seemed closer to the mark: a bird sitting on a wire that spelled out *believe*. The outline of a cat holding up her little paw and the word *persist*. I sent these images to Annabel, asking her what she thought.

"Are you really doing this?" she asked. "Is this the time I've heard about when the child becomes the parent?"

"Not yet. And yes, I'm doing it," I replied.

"Okay," she said. "But keep thinking. Those tattoos are a little basic, you know?"

I did know. Only because not long ago I was sitting with her brother Elias and a couple of his friends, visiting him at school in Boston, when they used the word *basic* about a girl they all were friends with. I asked what they meant by it. "It's nothing bad. It's just, you know, like a twenty-year-old in Starbucks who wears UGGs and Lululemon yoga pants and drinks pumpkin lattes. Basic." I still wasn't really getting it because, honestly, that all sounded great to me. I only understood the full meaning later when I was back at my hotel. I went down to the bar, where the clientele was too young for me not to be noticed. When the bartender asked what she could get me, I ordered a chardonnay and a kale salad with grilled chicken, which I then took up to my room so I wouldn't miss Rachel Maddow—it was then I realized for a white woman in her fifties, I was as basic as basic gets.

Maybe that's my tattoo: a tramp stamp that just says *basic*.

I could do something for my children, a nest with three little eggs. Or an empty nest. No, too sad. And enough about them. Not everything has to be for them. I'm a person separate from them, aren't I? Am I?

I remembered my friend, a hospice chaplain, saying everyone should have *DNR* tattooed on their chests so the paramedics know you don't wish to have extraordinary lifesaving measures performed should you keel over in your kitchen and not have anyone around to make your wishes known. Good sensible idea, but no. *No*. This tattoo was about identity, not death. How about a typewriter? A pen. The state of California. A dog paw. Comedy and tragedy masks. A chicken. How about the sun? Everyone likes the sun. But skin cancer. The moon. Who am I?

Okay, so maybe not a picture. Maybe a word. If there were one word that summed me up it would be . . . hungry. Hot—not as in sexy, just overheated. How about cranky? This is why I never got a personalized license plate. You see those ones that make you want to rear end someone, like LV2ACT, HTBLND, BSTMMY, FACEDR, or SXYMRS. My tattoo can't be braggy or nerdy or punny or pompous. Maybe it should be aspirational. The person I want to be. Warrior. Or Zen. Desperado. Maybe something in a foreign language. A haiku. Or the Sanskrit word for justice. Because I'm all about justice. How about just not do it? But it was too late. I already had the appointment. And more than that, the challenge of finding my word or picture or phrase felt suddenly necessary. I must stand for something. I wanted to ask someone who really knew me what they thought I stood for, but I was afraid of what they might say. Most people are not very self-aware, and I suddenly wasn't sure if I fell into that category as well.

I have a friend who's always saying, "You know me; I hate confrontation." This is someone who on any given day is feuding with the majority of her friend pool from elementary school through the present. There is no person I have had more conflict with in my entire life than this person who hates confrontation.

I have a sickly friend who swears every time she comes down with something that "it's so weird; I'm never sick." Or the several raging narcissists in my family who are "just sick of doing everything for everybody else all the time." Which leads me to wonder what delusions I'm harboring.

Also, I was going to have to think very seriously about placement. Getting a tattoo in your fifties is very different from getting one in your twenties. I had to avoid loose and crepey skin, which left me with only a few choice locations these days: my nose, the back of my neck, top of my foot, my shin, the palm of my hand, the side of my butt, the front of my thigh, the inside of my forearm, or my forehead.

Finally, the day of my appointment arrived, and I still hadn't landed on the perfect tattoo. Dayton, my youngest son, had some friends over. As I was leaving the house, he told them, "My mom's getting a tattoo today."

One of the girls said, "Oh. That's cool. What's it going to say?"

I said, "I'm thinking of a heart."

"Why?" another one of them asked.

"Because, you know, love," I said, lamely. They stared at me.

"Cool," the first girl said again. I could tell I was blushing, so I left. I certainly didn't need to explain myself to them. I certainly *couldn't* explain myself to them.

In the end, I went through with it. I decided on a tree. With my lucky number underneath. Because, you know, nature . . . and my lucky number. It's on the back of my neck, where I can't see it. I have to stand with my back to the bathroom mirror and take a picture with my phone, which I then have to zoom in on to see a blurry backward image of my new tattoo. It's not great. Most of the time nobody else will see it either because my hair will cover it, but I'll know it's there.

I sent the final result to Annabel, who wrote back, "You are a badass, Mom." I could not have asked for anything better than that. Except this, she wants to get a matching tattoo when she comes home for the summer.

My reaction was, "Absolutely not. Tattoos are trashy," exposing one of my delusions about myself. I would never have described myself as a hypocrite, but there you go.

I Don't Know Why I Say Hello

I've started to realize that my life has become a series of endless endings. My children's infrequent homecomings are all quickly followed by a relentless series of leavings. Their lives are about hellos right now, so they can't wait to untangle themselves from my octopus-like grasp and run out into the world that's so eager to greet them. Hello, love! Hello, Europe! Hello, career! Hello, world! For them it's all a beginning . . . and for me, it's nothing but goodbyes. Goodbye, bread. Goodbye, two-piece bathing suits. Goodbye, fried food, sleeveless shirts, skinny jeans, loud rock concerts, sun exposure, pregnancy scares, driving at night, eating at night, sleeping at night. Goodbye.

And then there are the final goodbyes coming in such rapid succession. I can't go on Facebook anymore without learning of the demise of at least a peripheral person in my universe who's dropped dead of what I guess we can no longer say are unexpected circumstances. You can't unexpect something that happens so often. Which has led to a low-grade depression that was hard to kick, which led to the decision that maybe *I* should say hello. To love. Well, if not hello, at least not fuck off to love. And so I got myself a boyfriend. Who was not a boy. Because I'm not a girl. We're both in our fifties—not even our early fifties. I suppose I could have dated a younger man to make me feel younger, but I suspect that would have only made me feel older.

The reason I bring up age as if it matters is because it does.

Starting a relationship at this time comes with a combined 115 years of life lessons and cautionary tales. We are both determined, even if it's only subconsciously, not to be brought down by the many, many mistakes of our pasts, and so the entire relationship becomes a Mexican standoff: the two of us eyeing each other carefully, waiting for the shoe to drop. Every time I go a little quiet, he's certain I'm formulating my breakup speech, just like I jump to the conclusion that when he says his apartment is too messy and he wants to fix it up a little before he invites me over, what he's really saying is "You can't come over because that's where my wife and three kids live." A little healthy paranoia is useful at this age, because fool us once, shame on us, fool us seven long-term relationships, three fiancés, four live-in boyfriends, and a nine-year marriage—what are we? Idiots? The answer is yes.

The first two months were filled with adorable discoveries of remarkable things we had in common: our favorite childhood TV show (*Flipper*), penchant for old Willie Nelson, hot dusty summers, horses, pet snakes, parents who didn't understand us, social anxiety, a dark sense of humor, a dream of escaping to a hundred acres on a river in a green valley. We marveled how more than fifty years could have gone by before happening upon a person who felt the same way we did about liverwurst (we love it). We told stories in the dark of our failed love affairs and dreams that died along the way. We shyly shared pieces of ourselves, hoping that the feeling of mutual admiration wouldn't evaporate once something concrete was presented, and even though we were both harsh critics, I could watch him sing and play guitar, and he could read what I wrote, and the bubble still didn't pop.

Our nervousness started dating the second month of our relationship. He was on the road, as he often is, being a touring musician—leave it to me to say hello to someone who is always saying goodbye—and he had stopped to see a friend in Tucson. I was vacationing with my kids in Vermont. We were negotiating our fresh romance long distance, through texts and brief phone calls. One evening, instead of sending his usual goodnight text, I got a terse two-word message: "Talk tomorrow." None of the usual Xs and Os, sounding an alarm from my supersensitive antennae, at which point my Damage whispered in my ear, "Something's wrong." My heart suddenly beat faster in my chest, my throat closed, my stomach rolled onto itself. *Uh-oh, uh-oh* were the only words that repeated in my brain. I had no evidence; nothing had actually happened. But my Damage is so attuned to a shift in energy that she's practically psychic. I didn't respond instantly; I had to play this right. I didn't want to lean in too far because if this was going south, the less I invested now, the less humiliated I would be and the more pride I could salvage at the end. Could this be the end? I had gone from perfectly fine just five minutes before to contemplating the end based on one text. That's how fast Damage works. Also, that's how bad texting is for long-distance relationships.

If I thought the I-love-yous came quickly at the beginning of this thing, that was nothing to how fast Damage could work her magic. So I waited a full thirty minutes before responding with a simple, "K." That's when *his* Nervous kicked into gear, and it wasn't long before another text arrived. His previously heartbroken hairs were obviously standing up on the back of his neck, too, so he tested the waters with an equally neutral message—nothing that would mark him as being the last one to reveal himself either—his Damage had played this game before as well. It was a photo of his friend's tortoise, eating a pile of lettuce. No caption. No commitment. His Damage just wanted to see if his assessment of the situation was correct—that we had taken a turn, there had been a cooling off. When I ignored that text, he was able to confirm what he suspected, and without so much as a conversation, our budding romance almost came to an end with four words and a picture of a reptile. And we both fell asleep, three thousand miles apart, on that.

When we spoke in the morning, things were revealed. What *I* didn't realize was that he had gotten stoned with his friend and, knowing my intolerance for being sober in a stoned conversation, decided to keep his interaction with me brief so as not to blow it. What *he* didn't realize was that lacking any other information, I automatically assumed his brevity meant he despised me. Because I lack object constancy. It's Freudian. See, Freud did an experiment where he played peekaboo with a bunch of babies. Some of those babies thought that was a great game and knew he was going to pop up any minute, so they waited in eager anticipation for him to return, smiles on their faces. But for some babies, every time he ducked and disappeared behind the wall or whatever, they thought he was gone forever, and they were devastated. They couldn't hold on to the idea of a person when he wasn't right in front of them. Probably because their parents locked them in the station wagon with a sleeve of Ritz crackers while they went into a casino in Reno to play slots . . . or something.

The point is, when someone goes away, the whole basis for the relationship suddenly feels like shifting sand, and we both spiraled down, sure that all was lost based on the thinnest possible evidence. Nervous dating Nervous. Damage dating Damage.

Combine that paranoia with the inescapable feeling that time is rushing past at a breakneck and heartbreaking pace, and we are operating with a sense of panic and hopelessness that has us grasping desperately at the greatness we see in each other while at the same time pushing each other away because of our post-romantic stress disorder, fatalistically certain that we're doomed—because why should this time be any different? Put it all together, and it's a fucking shit storm. Now add menopause to the equation, which leaves me with only two operating speeds—rage and despair—and you do not have the makings of a classic love story. It's not relaxing. And it's no one's fault. But at least we have each other. I think. I haven't heard from him all day.

Chasing Nothing

On August 26, I dropped my third, youngest, and final child off at college. To get there, we took a ten-day cross-country road trip from California to Vermont, our 4Runner loaded with his necessities and our two dogs, pulling my beloved 1963 Shasta camper behind us. We scheduled a meandering itinerary lined with fly-fishing meccas, scenic routes, and roadside attractions. We camped next to the Snake River, climbed the Grand Tetons, stopped at Mount Rushmore. We snacked on beef jerky and dill pickle–flavored sunflower seeds. We listened to Bonnie Raitt, Jim Croce, Prince, John Denver, James Taylor, Eminem, and Bob Dylan. Sometimes I let him listen to the Band, and sometimes he let me listen to the Dixie Chicks.

At the campgrounds where we stopped each night, most of the other campers were traveling in giant RVs with satellite dishes, working toilets, fully equipped kitchens, and king-sized bedrooms. My little vintage canned ham had a tiny but comfortable bed in the back with a foam mattress and good sheets where I slept. Dayton pitched his tent not far off. There was no bathroom in my camper, but some friends did give me a You Go Girl for Christmas, a rubbery funnel device that promised women the stand-up freedom of peeing only men had enjoyed until now. I hadn't quite mastered the You Go Girl yet—if you didn't get the angle just right, you'd Go Girl all over the floor of your camper, so I sometimes relied on a large red Solo cup instead when I got too spooked to walk to the faraway bathrooms or well-placed tree in the pitch-black night.

At the end of a long day of driving, Dayton usually set out to go fishing while I walked the dogs and chatted with other happy campers.

"Where you from?" they'd ask me from their lounge chairs, sipping their beverages from fancy plastic tumblers with double-insulated walls to keep their drinks cold, which I recognized and coveted from *Camping World* magazine.

"California. Me and my boy are driving cross-country."

"I like your rig," they'd say.

"Oh, thanks, yeah. Pretty comfortable for a tagalong."

"Did you do much reno?"

"Just popped in a double propane and updated the old icebox to a duel-fuel fridge."

That's how people talk on the road.

The kind of road warriors who are traveling with forty-foot motorhomes are usually parked for weeks at a time. Some of them stay in one location for the whole summer. Dayton and I would be moving on in the morning. We didn't even unhitch our camper from the truck so we'd always be ready to hit the road. I'd just make boiled instant coffee on the fire, and off we'd go.

We were very compatible traveling companions. Every time we passed a river or creek, I'd say, "You see that there, son? That's the mighty Mississipp" in the voice of an old-timey narrator. And every time I did, Dayton laughed. Every. Time. We had a lot of hours for good conversation. Somewhere in Utah, Dayton got the idea, "If I ever have a band, I'm going to call it Slim Pickins."

"That's already been a person," I told him.

He was disappointed. "There's no room left in the world for original thought," he concluded.

Somewhere in Idaho I yelled out, "I think that sign was just advertising a million acres for sale!"

"That's like a whole state," Dayton said, equally amazed.

"How would you put a fence around that?"

Dayton said you'd probably just get a force field. "If you can afford a million acres, you can definitely afford a force field."

I agreed.

There was a town in Illinois called Edwards. With a creek called Kickapoo. When we passed a road called Kickapoo Edwards, I told Dayton I was going to start introducing myself at the campgrounds that way. "How do you do? I'm Kickapoo Edwards. This is my boy, Big Poo."

Dayton was all for it. Because that's how Dayton is. Sometimes we didn't talk for miles. And that was good too. We might be soul mates. Don't tell him I said that.

I jokingly (not jokingly) said several times during our trip, "What if you didn't go to college? What if we just stayed on the road and see where it takes us?"

"No thanks," he said, not unkindly but firmly. Truth is, I'm fine with him going to college. He's ready. I'm ready. It's great to have this one last hurrah, but then it's time for whatever comes next. I'm fine with that. I am. I'm fine. I am.

When we pulled up to our campground in Chamberlain, South Dakota, at the end of day seven, the weather had turned ugly. Our spot overlooked the Missouri River, which was empty of summer boat traffic and churning with whitecaps.

As we were driving in, most of the other campers were pulling out, news of the approaching lightning storm sending them to hotel rooms for the night. Dayton and I decided to wait and see how bad it was going to get.

We pulled the cooler and other things out of the 4Runner to get ready for a quick dinner before the rain started. I told Dayton I didn't think it would be safe for him to sleep outside, but he ignored my advice and tried to put up his tent anyway, arguing there wasn't enough room in the camper. I watched as the wind almost took the tent from his hands and blew it right into the river. He caught it at the last minute and stubbornly tried to wrestle it to the ground until the lady who ran the campground drove up to us in a golf cart. She said there were tornado warnings and we should keep an eye out. If things got too bad, we would need to take shelter in the campground bathrooms. She stared at our California license plates with a final warning. "If you hear the sirens, don't fool around. The wind'll start blowing so hard you'll have to get your butt cheeks sewed back together." Then she drove away. Dayton and I stared at each other, then the rain started to fall.

He gave up on the tent. I told him we needed to get all of our equipment back into the 4Runner so it didn't blow away. I said I was going to put the chock blocks under the wheels of the camper so it didn't roll, then make a bed for him inside. I asked Dayton to put the cooler and other loose things back into the truck. After I got the blocks under the tires, I went into the camper. I flattened out the little kitchen table into a small second bed and arranged the seat cushions over the top. I put on the sheets, spread out a comforter, and threw on a couple of pillows, and it didn't look too bad. *Cozy*, I thought.

I lit the battery-operated lanterns, one near Dayton's bed and one at the head of mine on the other side of the camper, five feet away. I could tell the wind had picked up and the rain was coming down harder because the camper was rocking, but so far no water was coming inside. I was really hoping it remained dry—the Shasta had never been tested in a big storm, and she was fifty-two years old—just two years younger than me, and *I* certainly couldn't be considered impermeable.

I went to see how Dayton was coming along outside. I stood in the doorway and saw that the sky had turned black and thunder could be heard in the distance. The rain was steady. Dayton appeared to be moving in slow motion, carrying one item at a time from the picnic table to the open hatchback of the 4Runner. Then he stopped, with one hiking boot in his hand, and started turning in circles looking for the other one. I yelled at him from the doorway of the camper, like Auntie Em calling for Dorothy, startling him out of his daze, "Dayton! You have to hurry!"

He looked up at me. "What?"

"Hurry!" I screamed.

"I am," he said, standing perfectly still, forgetting what he was looking for.

"Move!" I shouted.

I looked at the horizon just as a giant-ass lightning bolt cracked through the heavens like a cartoon lighting up the dark sky and black river below. It was followed seconds later by a deafening clap of thunder. The two dogs and I almost jumped out of our skins, but Dayton still didn't spring into action.

Dayton asked, "Do you want everything in the car?"

I lost it. "Yes! Yes! Jesus!" I shrieked at him. "It's a tornado warning, for fuck's sake! Are you kidding me? Drop the boot and get in here! That's it. Fuck it. I am not leaving you alone at college if you're too goddamn stupid to come in when there's a tornado heading toward you. You're fucking staying with me! We're going back home tomorrow!" As soon as I finished screeching, I knew it was too much. But in my defense . . . tornado!

Dayton stared at me for a beat, then grabbed the rest of the stuff off of the ground, threw it into the back of the truck, and slammed the hatchback closed. He stomped toward me. I stepped out of his way. When he angrily boarded the camper, the whole thing rocked to the side in spite of my stability blocks. He threw off his wet jacket, flung it to the floor, and laid down on his kitchen table bed. It wasn't quite big enough for his tall frame, so he had to scrunch into it, but still he managed to turn his back to me. Then he called his dog to him. Canelo jumped on top of him, soaking wet with muddy paws. I almost yelled again, but I stopped myself. There was a moment when only the considerable noise from the whipping wind, rain, and occasional thunder filled the camper.

I had to yell again to be heard over it. I said, "I'm sorry." He didn't answer. I offered, "You can have a beer if you want one." Nothing.

Then with his back still turned, he said, "I'm not too stupid to stay alive. And I'm not staying home with you."

"Obviously, I know that," I said, too quiet to be heard.

I laid down in my bed. My golden retriever, Cabot, also soaking wet and stinking, immediately jumped up to join me, and we looked out the little back window that was facing the now raging river. We watched the lightning and pouring rain. Cabot shivered every time the thunder boomed. I tried not to think about how much I had to pee.

Sometimes you think you're fine. And then it turns out you're not fine. The problem was, I'd been keeping them all alive for more than eighteen years. It's pretty fucking insulting to think they could do it without me.

We fell asleep and woke up in the same place. We didn't fly away in the middle of the night and didn't wake up in the Land of Oz. The campground was a mess, but Dayton and I were back to normal. We didn't talk about it. We drank our boiled coffee and hit the road.

Two days later, the road ended at the university where Dayton would be starting his freshman year. It ended with me making his bed in his triple suite, assembling the storage containers ordered from Bed Bath & Beyond, hanging the California flag over his desk, arranging photos on his bulletin board of his pets, his brother and sister, his dad, and one particularly large and lovely shot of him and me that I was pretty sure would be taken down the minute I left campus because we kind of looked like a couple.

When I had organized, folded, fussed, and interior decorated as much as was humanly possible in the ten-by-eight-foot living space he was allotted for his freshman year, there was nothing to do but say goodbye. I gave my six-foot-two lumberjack man-baby a hard hug and wished him well. My throat was closing up, and we both knew I had to get out of there fast. I said something like, "You have to call me. And answer me when I text you. Right away or I'll think you're dead."

To which he replied, "I'll be careful, Kickapoo."

I ran out before my tears fell over my lower eyelashes and the biting of the insides of my cheeks stopped holding back the hiccup sob that was waiting to escape. I rushed past a security guard who was making sure nobody left their moving boxes where they didn't belong—and she very kindly averted her eyes.

I ran to the 4Runner, past the other parents telling their children to stay off drugs, and locked myself inside. I only cried for a minute. Just a momentary wave, because after all, this was the moment I'd been waiting for. And then I drove away, alone, on the nearly empty road, the two and a half hours to my house in Vermont. The place of my dreams. The one I'd fantasized escaping to when my days of school drop-off lines, jazz concerts, sporting events, theater productions, safety assemblies, parent socials, grad night committee meetings, annual picnics, Earth Days, world music nights, parent education seminars,

SAT practice tests, tutors, science camp drop-offs, college tours, college applications, winter formals, spring formals, tennis lessons, saxophone lessons, orthodontist appointments, wisdom teeth, ADHD testing, genius testing, grocery shopping, club soccer driving, community service forcing, fourteen-hour-a-day nagging, short-order cooking, monthly trips to the body shop days were over.

It also happened to be my fifty-fifth birthday. I've never been one to make a fuss over my own birthday. In fact, birthday celebrations have become a pretty reliable indicator for me when it comes to determining *my kind* of people. My kind of people celebrate other people's birthdays. *Not my kind* of people spend a lot of time celebrating their own. But for this particular birthday, it probably would have served me well to make even the smallest of plans for myself on my first night as an empty nester instead of digging into the boxed wine from my camper trailer at four o'clock in the afternoon and tuning into the *Criminal Minds* marathon. Watching hour after hour of Mandy Patinkin try to comprehend the evil in the world while crazy people found new and crazier ways to lop off (mostly) women's body parts was a dark way to usher in a new year and begin a new life chapter.

Sitting there, surrounded by nature and nothing else, I started to realize a few things. The first was how really far away the refrigerator was from the TV room, so finally I just brought the box of wine into the TV room, which could have been the beginning of a really bad birthday and definite downward spiral.

The second thing I realized was, as with most of my fantasies, I hadn't really thought this "take a break from work, no kids, live alone in the woods, and think about stuff" thing through. It was the same with my fantasy in high school about falling in love with an escaped prisoner. I lived in Chino, a town with four prisons. At my high school, we didn't have fire drills; we had prison break drills. When the alarm sounded, everyone had to walk single file out to the parking lot and board buses, which would then take us home, so the prisoners couldn't take the school hostage, I guess. Sometimes the sheriff's department would show up on our back road with dogs searching for the escapee. My fantasy was that when I went down near the back road to feed my horse, I would find the wanted, desperate, and handsome prisoner hiding in the shed where we kept the horse feed. He would pull me into the shed and force me to be quiet, maybe by kissing me . . . I don't know. Anyway, the prisoner would explain that he was 100 percent innocent of his crimes, and so I would agree to help him hide. I would keep him there, bringing him food in my tube top and overalls, and we would fall in love. And somehow while we were falling in love in my backyard, the police would discover he was innocent, and we would live happily ever after. Fortunately for me, I never came face-to-face with any of the escaped prisoners because I'm pretty sure none of them were innocent. Or handsome.

And now, here I was, alone in the middle of the woods in Vermont, and for the first time in more than twenty years, I didn't have a writing job on a TV show, a deal with a studio, or a child at home. I didn't have a boyfriend or any hobbies to speak of. I didn't play an instrument or knit. I had a couple of friends in Vermont, but they had jobs. They weren't really available to hang out with me all day. So what the fuck was I going to do with all my *freedom*? What did I do now with this person whom my children raised?

I turned off the gruesome television and sat in front of the window, looking at the miles of emptiness. Was I really going to have to have another fucking coming-of-age moment? Even at this age, when I had to wear glasses into the shower so I could tell which bottle was the shampoo and which was the conditioner? I spent my teens chasing friends and money and boys and a personality that suited me. I spent my twenties chasing love and money and fame. I spent my thirties chasing babies and money and success. I spent my forties chasing self-respect and balance and money. What would I chase in my fifties and beyond?

I was done chasing money. Because I know that too much money, like too much porn, can only squash your joy. As far as porn goes, anything your mind can imagine is available to you, as I once explained to my horrified young boys. You can watch women with men. Women with women. Men with men. Two women with two men. Spanking, sucking, bondage, bestiality, old ladies, big ladies, nurses, aliens, people dressed up like babies, cowboys, robots . . . "We get it, we get it!" my poor boys screamed, closing their eyes and covering their ears. My point was, just because you can access it with the click of a mouse doesn't mean you should. Because once you see everything there is to see, it's pretty likely that the simple joy of a naked boob is no longer going to do you any good at all. And that would be a shame.

People with too much money have the same problem. They wouldn't be able to find joy in discovering a long-lost Chap-Stick in a coat pocket they haven't worn for two years. The staff would have found that a long time ago. They also wouldn't be wearing a two-year-old coat. The overly rich no longer remember the thrill of going into the supermarket and being able to afford specialty salads. I was poor recently enough to still get a little wave of dread when the waitress took my credit card at a nice restaurant, waiting to see if it was going to go through. And to get a little rush of excitement when it did go through. I would hate to lose that. So I wouldn't chase money.

I wouldn't chase love, either. Love seems only to run away when you chase it. I think I caught my self-respect a little while ago. I had no interest in fame, which seemed like a drag. Maybe there was really nothing left to chase. Maybe I would just sit here for a minute or a month and see what came to me.

And that was the third thing I realized. It's possible I have everything I need. I have my ChapStick, my chickens, and my fine, funny children—all three of whom remembered to call me on my birthday.

Sometimes They Come Back

When your kids graduate from college and start their journey into the world, finally ready to put their education and life skills to good use, sometimes something happens while they're figuring it all out. While they're weighing their options and opportunities and sorting through the confusion of their early twenties, sometimes they come back.

Elias had been working on a campaign in Iowa for the midterms, and when that was over, while he looked for his next election, he came back home. Back to his old bedroom. Back to leaving dirty dishes on his nightstand and forgetting to put the alarm on when he returned home at 2:00 a.m. Back to sleeping in until one in the afternoon and complaining that I'm a loud walker early in the morning. Back to only using a towel for one forty-minute shower and then leaving it on the wood floor instead of hanging it for a second use, prompting me to consider printing up some of those hotel cards pleading for him to consider the planet and reuse towels rather than have housekeeping replace them daily. Back to eating the leftover fried rice that I had dreamed about having for breakfast. Back to turning down my requests for company on dog walks and movies, shopping trips and meals out. When I ask him what time he'll be home, I'm informed that he's an adult now and not required to apprise me of his comings and goings. So I'm back to sleepless nights, waiting to hear his car in the driveway, sneaking into his room every hour or so to look and see if that's a body in his bed or just the pile of crumpled sheets and discarded clothing he left behind when he went out to who knows where with God knows whom. My home has once again been transformed.

Not too long ago it was a lonely, empty nest that over time became a solitary but tranquil, very tidy haven. Now it has developed into a hostage crisis. Every once in a while, the sullen troll will emerge from under the bridge in the afternoon, grab a can of beer along with my newly purchased tub of Trader Joe's hummus and my very favorite sesame crackers, then disappear back into his lair. He doesn't speak or even make eye contact. He's going through a thing. So *we're* going through a thing. It leads me to think about what I was doing in my early twenties—none of it good—and that it wasn't anything a parent should bear witness to.

Friends advise me that it's temporary. It's a hard phase, this launch period, and a little time to regroup is not so much to ask, they say. He's putting *feelers* out, they say. "But he never comes out of his room!" I whine. Everything's done on computers now, they say. So I say nothing. But when I realize that what I thought was a thumb drive sticking out of his laptop, downloading what I thought must be his résumé, being sent out to what I thought must be his next career prospects, but was instead a USB-charged vape cigarette, I had to speak up. I don't know what a vape cigarette is exactly, but I keep seeing ads on the sides of buses warning that they are very dangerous and we shouldn't be kidding ourselves about their harmful effects. And there was also something on NPR about how these companies are marketing them to children with fruit flavors and they get them hooked and they have as much nicotine as cigarettes and might cause something called wet lung or popcorn lungs or cancer.

They've banned them in San Francisco, and San Francisco is right about everything! Besides, I quit smoking the day I found out I was pregnant with him, which I think gives me the right to an opinion.

I come into his room, a little more aggressively than I mean to, my voice a little more confrontational than I mean for it to be, because I'm scared, I realize. I mean, maybe the bed and the vaping are warning signs that something really bad is going on with him, so I say loudly and abruptly, "Are you still going to the gym?"

To which he replies, "Yes. I'm there right now," without looking at me. When I don't back away from the threshold of his room, which smells like a combination of ramen, bad man deodorant, and old beer, he looks at me, not patiently, and says, "Mom, I've been working eighteen-hour days for eleven months. I'm taking a break." I bite my tongue before I mention I've been working eighteen-hour days for forty years and I'm still waiting for my break because nobody likes a martyr. Unfortunately.

Again, I'm thinking about myself at twenty-two. Drinking too much, smoking too much. Making terrible decisions with terrible people that led to terrible mistakes. It was only because I was too broke that I didn't succeed as a serious drug addict. And it was with that regret and shame that I did everything I could to make sure my kids had not just opportunities but a safety net to ensure they didn't lose themselves, like I did, and had the tools to stay on track, like I didn't.

When they're babies, you think all you have to do is get past the time when they're hurtling toward every sharp corner that wants to take out their eye. Just make it to the point where they can no longer drown in an inch of water, and you'll be fine. But then you have to worry about some creep pulling up in a van and offering to show them a puppy so he can snatch them away. Then there's the drugs that appear in junior high, and now the lurking depression waiting for them in their twenties . . . thirty was no picnic . . . *I don't want him to get divorced in his forties!*

Okay. I know. I'm getting ahead of myself. First thing: get him out of bed. I don't know why, but the expression "idle hands make the devil's work" keeps popping into my head. My panic is turning me into Piper Laurie from the movie *Carrie.*

"If you're bored," I say, "and you want to earn some money, I could give you a few things to do around here."

"I'm not bored, but what kind of things?"

"You could go to the hardware store and replace the latches on the fences. All the screws are stripped."

"No, I don't really want to do that."

"You could take my car in and get that tire replaced for me."

"No, thanks."

"Well," I say, acting hesitant, "there is one thing . . . I mean, I kind of wanted to do this myself, but . . ."

He is looking at me, possibly vaguely interested.

"The porch needs to be restained."

"What do I have to do?" Aha, I think I just Tom Sawyer-d him into getting off the vape pipe and being a productive citizen.

I start to give him a list of supplies. "You're going to need some tarps to lay on the concrete—"

"I don't need those," he says. "I'll just be careful not to spill."

He also says he doesn't need to masking tape the molding; he's pretty good at painting straight lines. Or small brushes for the corners or sandpaper or rags or coveralls. His whole plan is just to rush in there and start rolling out deck stain willy-nilly, slapping on color without so much as a pressure wash or spackle. The only thing he says he needs is a long extension cord so he can bring his speaker outside for music. Finally, feeling a little lightheaded from his sheer cluelessness, I say I'll go to the store and get the supplies. He seems fine with that and crawls back into his bed while I head out to Lowe's.

Two hours later, when I come back, loaded down with the proper supplies, he's sound asleep. I wake him up with a hard poke to the back. Which makes him mad. But I'm mad, too, so tough shit. I follow him out to the porch, resisting my urge to kick him. He spends ten minutes carefully positioning his speaker, then pops open the five-gallon container of deck paint and is about to dip the roller inside, when I scream, "Stop! You have to stir it! Then pour it into a tray and roll it from there."

He picks up the paint stirrer stick, glaring at me, then moves it around a few times inside the tub of paint. When he pulls it out, some paint goes flying, several drips landing on the concrete.

"That's why you need to put the tarps down!" I shriek.

Elias drops the stick into the paint and looks at me. "Are you going to be standing out here the whole time? Because if you are, I'm not doing this."

Trying to sound reasonable (because I believe in my heart I am), I say, "I am employing you. I believe I have a right to a job well done. You haven't even swept the porch off yet, and you're about to just slap some paint down on it, which means all the little pieces of crap on the porch will get permanently painted into the surface."

"So?"

"So you just can't paint like this! Just not caring about anything. Rolling over cat hair and dead bugs. What are you doing with your life? I mean, it's like everything I've been saying to you since you were two years old hasn't gotten through at all. About being careful. And taking care of your body. About our family and addiction and how it's basically like you're walking around with a loaded gun! And how paint preparation is the most important step of all!"

I'm practically hyperventilating.

That's when Elias explodes.

"Stop! Just stop, okay? I can't take it anymore. You need to back off and let me live! You are way too much in my business, and you need to let me be! I hear you peeking in my room at night. I feel you watching what I'm eating. Looking at what I'm drinking! Let me do it my way! You are not right about everything all the time! I don't care what you think! I am not you!"

And then he storms off. His pants catch the end of the stirrer stick and a little more paint flicks onto the concrete (where there aren't any tarps laid down). And one small blob hits my favorite jeans. I hear the door to his bedroom slam. Then I hear the TV turn on. And that's it. I stand there for a minute.

Thinking about what just happened. How I wish I'd stuck to talking about painting. But also marveling because I find it very curious when you tell someone to butt out of your life, when you make a big showing of "I am an adult who needs my space, and you need to let me be, I've had it!" kind of speech, isn't that the part where you walk out the front door, get in your car, and go someplace? Do you walk back into your bedroom, snuggle under the covers, and wait for dinner? Do these kids not know how to tell someone to fuck off? When I told my parents to fuck off, I got into my Volkswagen Beetle, zoomed out of their driveway, found myself a boyfriend with a sister with a couch on the boardwalk in Venice, and didn't call for seven months. But he's not me. Which, I guess, is his point.

The next morning, Elias is up early, music blasting on the porch, vape pen sitting on the railing next to a cup of coffee. He rolls the paint onto the boards, not starting at one end and working his way across in a logical manner—but beginning directly in the middle and painting out in a circle until it reaches the edges, like a madman. By afternoon, he's done. It goes fast because he doesn't prime. And it looks good. Not perfect. But good. Especially once I put the indoor/outdoor rug down and the patio furniture. And, I mean, let's be honest: once the cat pees out there, who's really going to notice if there's a little paint on the molding? Maybe letting him do things his way isn't as scary as it feels. And letting go doesn't necessarily mean catastrophe will follow. He's not me. Thank God. I pay him something in the neighborhood of $140 an hour so he won't be mad at me anymore. He picks up his speaker and goes back to his room to continue going through his thing. I start cleaning up the painting supplies and continue to talk to myself—which, I guess, is now "my thing."

Two weeks later, Elias gets a job as field director for a cool woman running for a senate seat in Virginia. He packs up his car and leaves the next day to drive across country. As I watch him pull away to go make the world a better place, I realize he's everything I dreamed he would be. The house and the hummus are once again my own. I hate it.

Live Like You're Dying (You Are)

I'm dying. I realized it last week when the seat of my jeans gave way in the freezer section of the supermarket. I was browsing the frozen meals, deciding between a gluten-free cauliflower crust pizza or family-size Stouffer's mac and cheese, when I suddenly felt a draft across my lower butt. I poked around the underside of my fifteen-year-old favorite pair of jeans and discovered the seat had virtually disintegrated to the point that no further patchwork or desperate stitching would hold them together. When I got home, I had to break down and order a new pair of designer slim-fit boyfriend-cut button-fly jeans. When the new ones arrived, it occurred to me: if this pair manages to last for another fifteen years, I will be nearly seventy-five years old when this seat disintegrates. Meaning this could very well be the final pair of jeans I will purchase in my lifetime. And when I think about the fact that my time on earth is possibly only as long as the life-span of one pair of overpriced jeans, I fall into a panic that tells me I must hurry up. Hurry up and live because I'm about to die. And with so little time left, I need to make these years count. I need to do things that are worthwhile and life affirming and important.

And then I sit down on the couch and binge-watch *Forensic Files.*

I'm sure this will sound insensitive to people who really do die young, leaving so many things left undone. And here I am, alive and quite possibly with an abundance of time left to go—fifteen years is not nothing, I know. When my sister was dying at forty-one, she was furious about all the amazing things she wanted to do with her life that she was being denied. And if she were here right now, I would say to her, "Like what?" and "Do you have any ideas for me?" There's got to be something more to these remaining years than work, restorative yoga, Fitbit challenges, elimination diets, and skin cancer checks.

Maybe I should open a vegetarian restaurant. Except I'm not a vegetarian, and I have Misophonia—meaning I get unreasonably angry when I hear people chew. I could open a farm sanctuary, like Jon Stewart and his wife, Tracey. That's noble. When I start to look into it, though, I discover it can take years of paperwork to get the permits, and I don't have that kind of time or attention span.

Parenting felt worthwhile, but since the kids got jobs, they don't call as much. Why did I think I'd be happy when they were self-sufficient? It's made me obsolete. There are no more frantic messages about unjust parking tickets, cell phones dropped in rivers, overdrawn bank accounts. No more questions that only I knew the answers to: What is my social security number? Health insurance carrier? Where do you get stamps? How much do stamps cost? Why do I have a headache? Why does my tooth hurt? How long does it take to drive to New York from Boston? How long does it take for Advil to work? I was Alexa before Alexa. They are handling things on their own now, and I have lost my purpose. I need to find a new one.

I search the internet for things like "Impressive things to do with yourself after fifty," "Admirable life goals," and "What should I do now?"

I tried looking up what other empty-nest women I admire are doing with themselves these days: Michelle Obama, Hillary Clinton, Ruth Bader Ginsberg, Cher . . . very inspirational, but they're always out giving speeches and being honored, and I think I'd like to find something noble that I could do from home.

I talk to my friend Jackie about my plight—but she still has two kids at home and a full-time job, so she's only half listening.

I say, "I need something to do. Not just work. I need a purpose."

"I thought you wanted a pig."

"I'm saying I need a reason to get up in the morning. I don't have to change the world necessarily. Just a small purpose."

Jackie says, "I've never heard of small porpoises."

"Small purposes."

"Why are they small? Do they live with regular-sized porpoises?"

I know I don't have any more time to squander. I got a late start in life. While others were studying for the SAT in high school, their brains focused on their educational future, I spent my time watching and rewatching *Grease*, trying to decide if I was a Sandy or a Rizzo. Then, that first year away from home, while my peers were navigating their new academic environment, I was waiting for auditions, smoking Virginia Slims, drinking Miller Lites, and memorizing all the lyrics to the long version of Sugarhill Gang's "Rapper's Delight" (definitely a Rizzo).

When parents ask me to talk to their kids about how to get started as a professional writer, I tell them the truth: fail as an actress, don't prepare yourself to do anything practical, making yourself unhirable. This will ensure that you have to succeed or die. Also, be willing to be the butt of your own jokes. Somehow, and against all odds, that worked for me. And I was able to raise my kids with a certain amount of security. No one saw that coming, least of all me. And in the process, I transformed from an unreliable ne'er-do-well into a compulsive workaholic, super-mom, nonsmoker new person. But now what do I do with her?

Maybe I should run for office. No. Surely the roommate I had at nineteen would come out of the woodwork and reveal that I stole her sweaters when I moved out (I was a squanderer and sweater stealer). God! Why did I waste so much time? The voice in my head screams, *"Hurry! Hurry!* Figure it out! Do something!"

Then I sit down on the couch and binge-watch *Dateline.*

But even the soothing sounds of Keith Morrison's ghoulish narration can't quiet the voice in my head, whispering fiercely to "Go! Go!" and it has me scuttling to nowhere. I try to escape the anxiety by going to Vermont, sure that the lake and the trees and my kayak and the lack of panic-driven ambition in the people at Hasting's General Store will soothe me. But when I get there, I feel like someone who has come into the kitchen on a mission but can't remember why they went in there in the first place.

It's so peaceful and beautiful the only big idea that comes to me is this: "I'm going to have my ashes spread here." So I retrace my steps back to busier, less beautiful Los Angeles, where I can set up lunches and make appointments and possibly consult with a psychic.

I used to wake up in the morning like a starter's pistol had gone off. A script due, inbox and voice mail full of nagging emergencies. Running from producing to parenting. Trying to keep my show, *The New Adventures of Old Christine*—my work-child—alive; or during pilot season, trying to birth a new TV child; then rushing home to my real children, who were waiting for dinner to be cooked or last-minute school supplies to be magically pulled out of my ass because someone forgot to tell me they needed a three-quarter-inch two-ring binder in canary yellow by 7:00 a.m. tomorrow. Not anymore. The kids still haven't called me back. There are no emergencies. It's very quiet.

I'm all caught up on email, which wasn't hard because the only things in there were a special offer from the Sundance catalog, my Virgo horoscope from Astrology.com, a promo code from my pet food delivery service, the email from the porn site I put in my spam folder *every single day* only to be greeted by it again the next day, plus 472 requests for money from the Democratic National Committee. I turned in my latest script last week, four days early, because it was all I had to do. I don't have to multitask anymore, just task.

So I lie in bed, no alarm set, and orient for a few minutes . . . the only reason to get up is because the dogs and I have to pee.

What does one do when they can do whatever they want? I'm free. And I'm paralyzed by it. I'm dying. I'm free. I'm paralyzed.

My time is my own for the first time in many years, and while worry still waits at the edges of my thoughts (I'm still a mother), the hypervigilant state that I lived in while trying to give my kids everything they need while also building my career has relaxed. All three kids are on paths to productive adulthoods. I managed to steer them away from the pitfalls of my own misdirected youth. They are more secure than me in so many ways, which is all any parent can hope for. My career as a TV writer takes less desperate scrambling than it used to. I'm not quite an old-timer, but I might be a seasoned professional.

I look around at my clean, quiet, and orderly empty nest, french-pressed coffee waiting on the counter, a dozen eggs from my chickens waiting to be my morning omelet, and I realize this is not a tragedy. I can do whatever I please. It's like being twenty again but with better beer.

The years up till now have rushed by in a blur. It seems the pace of these next fifteen might slow to a crawl. And even though I have less time, I have more time. And doing nothing, for now, might be my midlife revenge. Maybe when the kids do finally call back, I won't even answer because I'll be resting on my laurels. I think I've found my Zen.

The first morning of my "I've done enough" lifestyle, I take the dogs for a walk. When we've gone a couple of blocks, I see a "Women for Trump" sign has appeared on a neighbor's lawn. I try to walk past it. Not my business. I'm done. Maybe I've done enough. I'm Zen.

We walk for a couple more blocks, and then I find myself turning back the way we came. Damn it.

I lead the two big dogs on either side of the sign as if I've lost control of them. Then I do a pretty good act (in case there are cameras watching) where I try to untangle the dog's leashes, only managing to wrap them around the sign. It turns into a fairly impressive physical comedy routine that ends up crushing the sign, dragging it down the street attached to my two dogs, then finally leaving it in a heap in the gutter. I couldn't help it. An American's work is never done. I'm nowhere near Zen.

I get back home, heart pumping with the exhilaration of crime, and there's a text message from my son. It's a picture of a rash, and the message says: "What do I do about this?" He needs me. I research the best-rated urgent care in the city where he's working, text it back to him with the directions and a copy of my medical insurance card. He sends back a thumbs-up and heart emoji. A mother's work is never done.

Small porpoises.

Happy, I sit down on my couch and binge-watch *Dr. G: Medical Examiner.*

Acknowledgments

I have to start with gratitude for Claudette Sutherland and everyone from the Wednesday morning table, because that's where it all started.

To Jennifer Kasius and the talented people at Running Press, your enthusiasm and wisdom made this process a joy. Thank you for your support and, most of all, for appreciating the fact that I am, at heart, a chicken lady.

To Megan Schindele and the eagle eyes at Amnet, thank you for curbing my comma addiction.

Thank you to my wonderful agents at CAA in New York: Mollie Glick and Anthony Matteo. You said you'd do it, and by god, you did.

Michael Rosenfeld, thank you for making what's important to me important to you. I believe that's the definition of a friend.

Brett Loncar, Jeff Jacobs, Jacquie Katz, and Michael Katcher, I realize you were hoping for a network sitcom, and instead I handed you scribblings from the inside of my uterus; the fact that you embraced it without missing a beat makes me feel lucky as can be to have you on my side.

Enormous appreciation to Karen Kim and everyone at Kessler, Schneider & Scheltinga for keeping the lights on.

Thank you to Bob Getman. You've been there for me for so long, I'm starting to count on you.

Scott Schwartz. Because.

I have truly amazing women in my life: Jackie, Rosie, Helen, Amy, Katie, Noodle, Jhoni, Elizabeth, Julia, Nancy, Heather, Julie, Mary, Tracy, and Kathleen. Don't ever leave me. I'm not kidding. Don't.

To my mom and dad, for teaching me to laugh inappropriately and often.

Casey, Lisa, Kady, Toby, Tricia, Wyatt, Poseidon—my family.

To Toby E.—a very welcome addition.

Matt, you came into the picture during the tornado. You can officially add storm chaser to your list of credentials. I love you.

To every animal that's saved me.

And to Annabel, Elias, and Dayton, for everything. All the time.